John Harrold

Libby, Andersonville, Florence

The Capture, Omprisonment, Escape and Rescue of John Harrold

John Harrold

Libby, Andersonville, Florence
The Capture, Omprisonment, Escape and Rescue of John Harrold

ISBN/EAN: 9783744761253

Printed in Europe, USA, Canada, Australia, Japan

Cover: Foto ©ninafisch / pixelio.de

More available books at **www.hansebooks.com**

LIBBY, ANDERSONVILLE, FLORENCE.

THE

CAPTURE,

IMPRISONMENT, ESCAPE AND RESCUE

OF

JOHN HARROLD,

A UNION SOLDIER IN THE WAR OF THE REBELLION.

WITH A DESCRIPTION OF PRISON LIFE AMONG THE REBELS
—THE TREATMENT OF UNION PRISONERS—
THEIR PRIVATIONS AND SUFFERINGS.

PHILADELPHIA:
WM. B. SELHEIMER, Printer, N. W. cor. Fifth and Chestnut Streets.
1870.

DEDICATED,

WITH RESPECT AND WARM FEELINGS OF GRATITUDE,

TO

General William T. Sherman,

MY DELIVERER,

WHO RESCUED ME IN MY FLIGHT FROM THE HORRIBLE PRISON
PEN OF FLORENCE, BROUGHT ME WITHIN THE LINES
OF THE UNION ARMY, AND ENABLED ME TO
REACH MY

HOME AND FAMILY IN SAFETY.

JOHN HARROLD.

INTRODUCTION.

I have often been solicited to publish the details of my experience in the army during the Rebellion, including an account of my capture, imprisonment, and the perilous incidents connected with my escape; but a feeling of diffidence long restrained me, until I reflected that the record of a father's services, in the trying scenes of that period, was the only legacy I could leave to my five boys—four of whom were born before I enlisted.

I shall enter into no description of the battles in which I participated, because I know that abler historians have performed that task better than I could. Nor can I give precise dates of all that occurred, from the fact that I was robbed of my diary by a rebel officer while a prisoner.

My ignorance of the country through which I traveled prevents me from naming counties or districts; and I could only guess at distances, except where I received information from others.

My purpose is, to give a plain and truthful narrative of facts as they occurred, and as they were seen from a soldier's stand-point. I might have added a great deal that was irrelevant, but none the less interesting, to this sketch, by commenting upon much that I saw and heard; but so much has been written by others that I deemed it unwise to make the attempt. I only seek to discharge a duty I owe to my children in penning this narrative; but if its perusal should serve to add to the pleasure of an idle hour, or give the public a higher appreciation of our citizen soldiery—their patriotism and devotion to the Union—it will prove as gratifying to myself as to my friends, who induced me to make the venture.

JOHN HARROLD.

Atlantic City, N. J.

THE Capture, Imprisonment, Escape and Rescue

OF

JOHN HARROLD.

CHAPTER I.

ENLISTMENT—DRILLING—PICKET DUTY.

In common with thousands who left home, family and friends, I responded to the call of President Lincoln for volunteers, in July, 1862. I was but a journeyman mechanic, with a wife and four small children dependent upon me for support. I confess I was unpleasantly situated to think of entering the army, and many pronounced me rash and thoughtless to leave them partially unprovided for; but, after consulting with my wife, whose patriotic feelings seemed to overcome all apprehensions, she gave a reluctant consent. "Wait till you are drafted," was the advice of many warm friends, as they pointed to a toiling mother and four almost helpless children.

This agreed with my notions of interest and comfort, but not with my sense of duty to my country. No matter what may be a man's position in life, he must be callous, indeed—dead to every patriotic impulse—if he can passively witness gigantic efforts to destroy this Union without extending an arm to save it.

Feeling thus, I made what provision I could for my family, and volunteered under the first call for three years' service—joining the 138th Pennsylvania Regiment, which was organized August 16th, 1862, at Harrisburg, under the command of Col. C. L. K. Sumwalt. I was enrolled in Company A, M. R. McClellan, captain.

From the 16th to the 30th of August, the regiment was drilling, equipping, and making the necessary arrangements to take the field, for which we started on the day last mentioned, and reached Baltimore on the 31st. Our colonel reported to Major General Wool, who assigned us to duty at the Relay House, known as the junction of the Washington and Baltimore and Ohio Railroads.

It was here that my first experience as a soldier commenced, by going on picket duty in regular order. In this capacity there is much of exposure, no little danger, and many privations to be endured,—including loss of sleep, hunger, wearing wet clothes, &c., all of which is readily comprehended by those familiar with a soldier's life. On one occasion, I was detailed, with some twenty others, for special duty of a confidential character. We accomplished all that was required of us to the satisfaction of our superior officers, and returned to our command in safety. But, in the nine months we remained at the Relay House, we had many pleasant seasons of relief, which we seldom found afterward. False alarms, the sudden call to arms, and the jokes incident to these "camp scares," afforded the "boys" no little amusement.

CHAPTER II.

ACTIVE DUTY — FLANKED — THE COUNTERMARCH — BATTLES OF WAPPING HEIGHTS, KELLY'S FORD AND BRANDY STATION.

After Lee's invasion of Pennsylvania, our regiment was transferred to Maryland Heights, where we began to realize a soldier's life in earnest. The nearer we approached the enemy, the more arduous became our duties, as a greater degree of vigilance and more severe discipline was necessarily exacted. We remained at this place two weeks, when we were transferred to the Third Division, Third Corps, commanded by Major General French, with Major General Meade as Commander-in-Chief, just in time to participate in the battle of Wapping Heights. I will not pause to describe this battle. It is enough to say that our regiment got the praise of "behaving admirably," and we thought we deserved it. I will not deny that I was timid and apprehensive as the chances of life and death were alternating in the struggle, for thoughts of my wife and children would intrude upon me; but the excitement, roar and confusion incident to battle soon chased away such feelings, and we gradually learned to become insensible to danger. After this "brush" we coun termarched to Warrington, and encamped at the Junction a few days, when we struck tents and moved to the North Branch of the Rappahannock, and encamped there some weeks. We were again ordered on the march, and proceeded to Culpepper, where we remained about two weeks. We moved from here some two miles, when an order came to countermarch; and that countermarch I shall never forget. Lee had flanked us, and we were compelled to fall back precipitately. The panic, the confusion and the scramble to escape that wily general's trap, can be better imagined than described. The soldier would sooner, by far, engage in a deadly conflict, than undergo the trials and vexations of a hasty retreat. On such occasions but little of discipline is observed, and man's selfish instincts are prominently developed. Self-preservation is the prevailing motive, and few pause to render help to those who are sick or disabled. Of course, there are exceptions, and noble ones, but, as a general thing, each man is for himself, and all cumbersome articles—some essential to the comfort of the soldier—are cast aside. Anything and everything that retards speed is thrown away—from the cartridge-box to the musket.

We reached Fairfax Station, however, after having partially recovered from the disorder into which the corps was thrown, and rested two days. From this point we followed the rebels back, and found they had torn up the Orange and Alexandria Railroad for some twenty miles.

This we repaired, and moved on to Kelly's Ford, where we participated in an animated fight, and captured a rebel regiment. From this point we moved on to Brandy Station, our regiment being placed on the extreme front of the corps. Here we encountered the "Johnnys" in strong force, with their artillery well posted. Our regiment was ordered to advance, and did so most nobly, amid a storm of "iron hail and leaden rain." After a fearful struggle, which was hotly contested by the rebels, we compelled them to make a hasty retreat; but not without the loss of one of our bravest officers, Captain L. C. Andress, of Company H,—a gentleman beloved and mourned by the entire regiment. Others, of course, shared a similar fate, and we had our share of wounded and missing.

After resting a few days, we were ordered to strike tents on the morning of the 23d of November, and we crossed the river at Jacob's Ford. After a long and wearisome march, we encountered the enemy in strong force at Locust Grove. Here a terrible battle was fought, lasting from 2 o'clock until after dark. Our regiment was long and warmly engaged, and our terrible loss attests the courage with which our men faced the foe. We lost sixty in killed and wounded, including our colonel, who was severely injured. My good fortune followed me throughout the entire conflict. I did not receive a scratch, although a number of my comrades fell around and near me. It would be impossible to portray the various scenes enacted, or to describe the different positions occupied by the troops. There is constant changing and manouvering, as circumstances may render expedient, and one description of a battle might answer for many. It may not be amiss, in this connection, to append the following picture of a battle scene, which appeared in print shortly after the war, and which will give the reader a better idea of its horrors:—

"Steadily the brave fellows ascended the range of hills, two ranks deep, under a furious fire of artillery, flashing death's terrors under the most fearful form, and gayly they climbed the numerous fences in their way. Men dropped, gaps were made in the ranks, but the lines were immediately closed—all were compact as before. The wounded silently fell. All bosh about the screams of the wounded that we read of in the books. On they went until a blazing fire of musketry stormed upon them from the rifle-pit hitherto invisible, and induced a halt. Firmly they stood and returned the fire. Up went the swords of the field officers, wildly cheering them on. Again they advanced. Again they halted. Line officers ran behind the men, picking up cartridge-boxes of the dead, and replenishing those of the living.

Back and forth they went, in the rear of their companions, asking men if their ammunition held out, indicating localities where shots might be effective, and encouraging them with hopeful words:

'Steady, boys, steady; give 'em thunder! Smith, are you hurt?'

'Yes, sir; my arm's broke.'

'Go to the rear, my boy.'

Another boy falls.

'Where are you struck, Robert?'

'In the thigh, sir. I can't move.'

'Lie still and keep cool; they'll take you away soon.'

'Dennis, what's the matter with you? Why the devil don't you fire?'

'The ball's banked to the top o' me muskit togither, sir, and broke the bagenet.'

'Pitch it away; here's another. Fire faster, Jones! That's right, Robinson! Give it to 'em! Splendid! boys, splendid! Down with you, a new battery opening.'

So it goes, encouragement and reproof by turns, in quantities varied by the individual vitality of the officers, interspersed with constant orders to lie down and avoid the fire of the batteries.

'D——n this knapsack! I can't stand it!' says one; and it is jerked off.

'This coat is as hot as ——,' says another, and off it goes.

Terrible is this work of death! The enemy in the rifle-pits have the advantage of three to one. They put their heads up, fire, and down they go to load.

'Oh, blast it! Cap'n, we ain't got no chance against them fellers; we ought to have reinforcements.'

This cry extends along the lines. Colonels, in their visits to their regiments, hear it from their line officers; soon it comes to the knowledge of the generals, and after an hour's fighting, an order to fall back is given, which is obeyed with a steady pace, and but little straggling."

We next moved to Mine Run, where we found the enemy strongly entrenched. The weather was intensely cold, and the rebels so well guarded against assault, that our commander wisely concluded to fall back. This we did in good order, although closely followed by Lee's forces. We succeeded in recrossing the Rapidan with the loss of a few prisoners, and encamped once more at Brandy Station, where we remained until the army was reorganized—performing picket duty, reconnoitering, and other service pertaining to camp life.

CHAPTER III.

THE ARMY REORGANIZED — GENERAL GRANT TAKES COMMAND — THE BATTLES OF THE WILDERNESS — "ON TO RICHMOND" — THE TERRIBLE CONFLICT AT COAL HARBOR.

While encamped here, the army was thoroughly reorganized by that great chieftain—who never knew defeat—General Grant. There had been such frequent changes of commanders that the soldiers began to grow distrustful. Each of those displaced had their admirers; and, say what you will, confidence in a general is an essential auxiliary to the firmness and bravery of an army. While many were loth to part with old favorites, few, if any, were unwilling to accord great merit to General Grant; and in view of the rapid dismissals and successions preceding his command, the Army of the Potomac gave him as hearty a welcome as could be expected under the circumstances.

Long before the fourth day of May, 1864, had dawned upon the hills of Virginia, the rolling of drums, and the shrill notes of the bugle, aroused the slumbering Army of the Potomac, and preparations were immediately commenced for the long expected movement. Winter quarters were promptly stripped of their appurtenances, and the troops were paraded under arms, and stood in readiness for the word of command. The following eloquent and stirring address of the Commanding General was then published to the army prior to the commencement of the march, which I feel called upon to embody in this narrative. I need not say that its words of caution, the confidence expressed, and the thrilling appeal made, in view of the great task before us, made a deep impression upon every patriotic mind, and all felt their force and importance:

HEAD-QUARTERS ARMY OF THE POTOMAC, }
May 4th, 1864. }

SOLDIERS!—Again you are called upon to advance against the enemies of your country. The time and the occasion are deemed opportune by your Commanding General to address you a few words of confidence and caution. You have been reorganized, strengthened, and fully equipped in every respect. You form part of the several armies of your country, the whole under the direction of an able and a distinguished General, who enjoys the confidence of the Government, the people and the army. Your movements, being in co-operation with others, it is of the utmost importance that no effort should be left unspared to make it successful.

SOLDIERS!—The eyes of the world are looking with anxious hope to the blow you are about to strike in the most sacred cause that ever called men to arms.

Remember your homes, your wives and your children! and bear in mind, that the sooner your enemies are overcome, the sooner you will be returned to enjoy the benefits and the blessings of peace. Bear with patience the hardships and sacrifices you will be called on to endure. Have confidence in your officers and in each other. Keep your ranks on the march and on the battle-field; and let each man earnestly implore God's blessing, and endeavor, by his thoughts and actions, to render himself worthy of the favor he seeks—with a clear conscience and strong arms, actuated by a high sense of duty to preserve the Government and the institutions handed down to us by our forefathers —if true to ourselves, *victory*, under God's blessing, must and will attend our efforts.

GEORGE G. MEADE,
Major-General Commanding.

On the morning of the 4th of May, therefore, the whole Grand Army of the Potomac was put in motion, and crossed the Rapidan at Martin's Ford. We advanced through the Wilderness, skirmishing, until we encountered the main body of Lee's army. A series of battles ensued from the Wilderness to Spotsylvania Court House, the enemy disputing every inch of ground, and fighting with a bravery worthy a better cause; but Yankee courage and perseverance admitted of no pause, and General Grant kept us constantly on the move. We drove the enemy from one entrenchment to another, defeating their best strategy in manouvering, and putting Lee's flanking tactics at defiance.

The carnage was terrible, and both armies were sadly depleted; but troops came pouring in from the North, and our numbers were kept pretty well up to the mark. I will not attempt to describe the perilous scenes through which I passed; that task belongs to the historian, and to that source the reader must look for particulars. Throughout all these engagements I was at my post, and in none of these sanguinary conflicts did I receive bodily injury worth mentioning. The miraculous escapes I made, even when men were falling one by one around me, seemed to inspire the belief that I should come out of the war unharmed; and this confidence in my "good luck," as soldiers term it, did much to render me cool and collected in time of battle. I need not say how thankful I felt for my preservation at the close of each conflict, and yet I could not but feel sad to see my comrades drop down, one after another, like leaves in autumn.

After nine days and nights of hard fighting, our commander issued a congratulatory address, informing us that we had driven the enemy from all his strongholds, stating the number of prisoners captured, and naming the advantages obtained, closing by calling upon us to be ready at a moment's warning for a forward march. The reader can imagine the condition we were in to resume hostilities. In all this time we were frequently without rations, and were compelled to endure hunger as well as fatigue. We could only take "cat-naps," as opportunity offered, on the ground, in the storm, standing or walking, for the exhausted soldier will sleep on foot as well as in the saddle.

The greatest annoyance, however, consisted in the irregularity of the supply trains. While on the advance, constantly fighting or pursuing, it is impossible for them to keep up. Indeed, it would be dangerous to do so; for, should any sudden reverse come upon us, they might prove a valuable prize to the enemy, if they did not prove an insuperable barrier to a safe retreat. Hence the necessity of keeping them a certain distance in the rear. Under such circumstances, parties are detailed to bring "hard tack" to the front, and deal it out in small parcels to the soldiers, when it is safe to do so.

We now took up our line of march, crossed the Pamunky river, on our way to Coal Harbor, and traveled two days and nights without rations, as the supply train failed to reach us. But, we knew that Gen. Grant's motto was "onward," and that we must move on with or without rations. We reached Coal Harbor about the 2d of June, where our cavalry was sorely pressed, and halted for the supply train to come up, as both our stomachs and haversacks were empty. We feasted on a soldier's fare, and slept, as only the weary can sleep, until 4 o'clock in the afternoon, when we were aroused and moved out about two miles, to the Coal Harbor and Richmond Turnpike.

Here we halted, commenced manouvering and forming in line of battle. The questions—"What's the matter?" "Where's the Johnny's?" &c., went along the line. Our curiosity, however, was soon satisfied; for I never witnessed as sudden and as terrible an onslaught as that made upon us by the enemy. It was like the shock of an earthquake— the ground trembled—cheeks paled that had been facing death in every shape for the past two weeks. Lips were compressed, and muskets grasped tighter, as this sure premonition of a hard struggle came upon us. As we formed in line our brigade was ordered to advance. We had scarcely crossed the Coal Harbor road, and penetrated the woods, when the enemy opened with musketry and artillery. The shot and shell came upon us like a hailstorm. The whiz-zoo-oo of the bullets, the rattle of grape, and the roar of shells—tearing up the earth and wrenching large limbs from trees, hurling them in all directions—added to the awful grandeur of the scene, and was well calculated to test the courage of the stoutest heart.

Our regiment, with the 6th Maryland, charged through a swamp waistband deep, and carried that portion of the enemy's works in front of us—capturing more prisoners than the aggregate number of men in both our regiments. This feat was performed while the storm of death raged around us, and not a man quailed or faltered, but one and all pressed on with an enthusiasm that seemed to rise proportionate to our dangerous surroundings. The attack of the enemy was so violent, and so simultaneous, that each man appeared to be impressed with the belief that the fate of the day depended upon his own individual exertions. Never did soldiers vie with each other more nobly in performing deeds of valor; never did I witness harder fighting. But, once more our glorious flag waved in triumph, and even the wounded and dying were consoled with the shouts of victory.

Again I escaped with a few slight scratches, which some might magnify into wounds, but they caused me but trifling inconvenience. Of course, I was in great peril on several occasions, and actually had a part of my moustache shaved off by a bullet. I have no disposition to glorify myself, or to play the hero on paper, therefore I shall not allude to my personal efforts on that day; but I consider it one of the proudest records of my life to have fought side by side with men whose valor and prowess made them heroes indeed. It was this battle, above all others, that dispirited the rebels, and must have convinced the intelligent portion of them that they were only struggling in a "lost cause."

CHAPTER IV.

PROMOTION—CAPTURE.

Here we held our ground and fortified strongly—continuing our operations at Coal Harbor from the 2d to the 12th of June. At this point I received the appointment, by detail, of Brigade Postmaster, in connection with that of the Regiment—a position I had held for some time. The new duties devolving upon me made it necessary to have the use of a horse; and I soon became master of a "bunch of bones" which bore a strong resemblance to the rider, as I was much reduced by the hardships I had passed through. I was kept on the move, however, having to visit many head-quarters frequently, to attend to mail matters for the brigade and regiment. I was often compelled to go to the Sanitary Commission Head-Quarters to get my mails, when I could not obtain them through the proper channel.

While at this post, about mid-day on the 12th of June, I discovered that the head-quarters of the army was broken up. I mounted my celebrated steed, known to the boys as "Rapidan," and which extorted many humorous comments upon both horse and rider, and started for the front, where I saw my Colonel, and asked him if he had received orders to move. He said he had orders to move back to some lines of entrenchments that had been erected that day. I inquired whether he thought a general movement was about to take place. He thought not, and was under the impression that a part of the army would move, and that our corps and the Second Corps would remain for a day or two. I asked for instructions, when he told me to remain at the Sanitary Commission Head-Quarters over night. I noticed that his servants, with the Majors and Adjutants, were in the rear with the horses, and he directed me to tell the former to have every thing ready in case a forward movement should be made, of which he would apprise me.

I rode back in company with the Commissary Sergeant of my regiment, delivered the Colonel's orders to his servants, made final arrangements for the night, and laid down to sleep. About 3 o'clock, A. M., I was aroused by a comrade, who informed me that the cavalry were passing. I jumped up, well knowing that it was the rear guard of the army. This was somewhat perplexing; but after consulting with my companion, it was decided that I should start out and endeavor to find my command, although we both considered it a pretty dangerous undertaking at such an hour. I mounted "Old Rapidan," and went about half a mile to an open space, where there had been a number of division and brigade head-quarters the evening previous, but everything had disappeared as if by magic.

In this dilemma I scarcely knew how to proceed, or what to do. I was bewildered, and tried to penetrate the darkness, but in vain. I heard picket firing in various directions, saw the camp-fires burning in the distance, and still I hesitated what course to pursue. I finally concluded to visit the new entrenchments. I had traveled about half a mile, when I paused to listen, and hearing pretty loud talking ahead of me, felt certain our men were there. I started off in a good round trot, and soon reached the vicinity of Old Coal Harbor Tavern. Here I was startled by voices apparently coming from the underbrush near me, and directly there came the stern command—

"Halt!"

My old horse was a disciplinarian, and instantly stopped. I confess I trembled with apprehension, as I knew not whether the command came from friend or foe. By the time I recovered my self-possession, I was surrounded by about twenty-five rebels. In a moment the bridle of my horse was seized, and three muskets leveled at my head.

"Dismount!" was the next imperative order, which I slowly obeyed; and mustering all the courage I could, resolved to make the best of my unpleasant situation. The examination began with:

"Hello, Yank, you're in the wrong box this time."

"I should judge so, sir."

"What are you?"

"I am a United States soldier, sir."

"What are you doing out here?"

"Looking for my command."

"Which way have they gone?"

"That is what I want to find out. What regiment do *you* belong to?"

"Sixteenth Alabama."

"You won't kill a fellow, will you?"

"Oh, no. Come along; we want to show you to our colonel."

Accordingly, I was taken before a long, lank, lean, rawboned Alabamian, with a most repulsive countenance, and a uniform a good deal the worse for wear. His first salutation was—

"Hello! who do you belong to?"

"To Uncle Sam, sir."

"What corps do you belong to?"

"The sixth, sir."

"Which way has the army moved?" (These questions were asked rapidly.)

"That is what I came out here, to my sorrow, to find out."

"Don't you *know* which way they have moved?"

"Even if I did, colonel, I should be very sorry to give you any information in regard to their movements. It would not look well in me to come out here and betray my own comrades."

"I will soon find out."

"I'll guarantee, sir, that General Grant will soon turn up somewhere."

Examining me from head to foot, and looking earnestly at my haversack, he asked—

"What have you got in that haversack?"

"Some letters and private effects of my own."

"I will take charge of them."

"That haversack," I replied, "is my own private property." It was a very neat patent-leather sack, and I was loth to part with it; but right was forced to yield to might.

"I want it."

"Colonel, that is the only thing I have left of any service to me. I hope you will permit me to retain it."

"He repeated, in a peremptory manner, "I want it," and I was forced to surrender what was to me a treasure indeed.

In the meantime, some thirty or forty persons were brought in, and the guard received orders to march us off to General Mahone's head-quarters, where we came to a halt, and was soon surrounded by a number of the most wretched-looking men I ever saw. Some of their uniforms resembled Joseph's coat, exhibiting patches of all colors, and well-ventilated at that. A more dirty, squalid, poverty-stricken set of soldiers I never saw assembled together. They had nothing but tobacco, which they offered to trade for finger rings, watches, buttons, &c. Soon a fine, noble-looking officer approached us, and, directing his conversation to me, remarked—

"Boys, you were caught napping this time."

"Yes, sir," I replied.

"Which way has your army gone?" (This appeared to be the leading question.)

"Captain, if I knew I should be loth to tell you."

"Oh, that is nothing."

"I know, sir, it is *nothing* more than acting the part of a traitor, and the informer would be guilty of treason."

"Have you any papers?"

"No, sir. I have nothing left but a diary."

"Let me see it."

To use an army phrase, I thought it was "gone up," and said, "do not deprive me of that. Colonel Saunders, commanding a brigade in General Mahone's division, took my haversack from me."

"Oh, he will give it back to you again."

"He gave me but little hope that I should ever see it again."

He commenced perusing my diary, and, after looking over it for some time, suddenly paused. Looking at me sternly, he said—

"Now, I want to ask you a question, and desire a candid answer. As a man of honor, I want you to give me an honest answer."

"If consistent with honor, I will."

"This is the question: Do you really think that General Grant gained any advantage over General Lee in the battle of the Wilderness, and up to the present time?"

"Captain, I am astonished at the question."

"Why?"

"I believe, as much as I believe I have an existence, that you would have kept us in the Wilderness nine years instead of nine days, if you could. We have driven you back to within seven miles of Richmond. If you could have prevented it, you certainly would."

"Oh, you are infatuated," he exclaimed, as he handed back my diary.

Our numbers were now increased to over forty. We were placed in a large barn, under guard, and well they performed their duty. Some of our men were in a sorry plight, having been plundered of hats, coats, boots, &c. We had been there but a short time, when a ragged, rough-looking fellow demanded our gum and woolen blankets, knapsacks, and every article we needed for personal comfort. One of the men told him we were prisoners of war, and did not know that we had fallen into the hands of highway robbers. This only provoked a volley of the most shocking oaths, asserting that the rebels "could lick the d———d Yankees any time." I told him he was very brave among unarmed men, and he could afford to exhaust his wrath upon us.

CHAPTER V.

STARTING FOR "LIBBY."

After being stripped and robbed of all save sufficient to cover us, we were ordered to "fall in," without a mouthful to eat. We marched over Gaines' Farm, across the Chickahominy, and over the celebrated McClellan Bridge, at Gaines' Mills—following up the rear of the rebel army—through the historic fields of Fair Oaks, and brought up in the rear of Longstreet's Corps. We turned to the left of the Fair Oaks' battle field into a direct road to Richmond—passing through some very formidable fortifications, guarded by the *elite* of the "chivalry." These were termed the "Home Guards," and were held in great contempt by the men at the front. Those who had seen service, while guarding us, gave us more freedom in our replies to any jeers or coarse jokes put upon us. But not so the "chivalry." As we entered the main defences of Richmond, these holiday soldiers would sing out "on to Richmond! on to Richmond!" One fancy fellow, with a flashy uniform, appeared very boisterous, and kept repeating the expression. "Oh, yes," I replied, "General Grant has detailed us to put up his Head-Quarters in Richmond." He almost exploded with rage, and uttered curses that I will not repeat here. "Why." said I, "that fellow looks as if he had just come out of a rifle-pit." This brought the laugh upon him from the old guard, and he hastily left amid their jeers.

We reached the suburbs of Richmond hungry and thirsty, and laid down to rest: but I was soon aroused by calls for the mail agent. I was asked for papers, and the usual inquiries were made in regard to the whereabouts of the army, &c., to all of which I replied as formerly. We were soon ordered to march, and proceeded through the streets to Libby Prison, entering the centre of the building. I confess I was agreeably disappointed in regard to its sanitary condition. The apartment we entered was very clean, with a long dining-table running through the centre, and a number of pipes conveying water to a bath-tub. We had eaten nothing since the evening previous, and seeing the table and other conveniences for meals, we naturally anticipated a speedy supply of rations; but, alas! we were doomed to cruel disappointment.

After performing our ablutions, we inquired of the guards for something to eat, but no attention was paid to our appeal. In about half an hour, and before we had gone through the process of cleansing our persons, an officer strutted in very pompously with a book under his arm, and with more gold lace upon him than a monarch's lacquey would wear. This was the notorious Dick Turner.

His first salutation was—"Fall in, you d——d yankee s——s of b——s." We obeyed quickly, not knowing what was to follow; but we soon found out to our sorrow. I had a watch and thirty-six dollars in money with me, and flattered myself that, as I had been suffered to retain this property so far, it would not be taken from me; but I was mistaken. My clothing, save all that was necessary to hide nakedness, my watch and money, were all taken from me by order of this robber; and I was left in this pitiful condition without a cent in my pocket.

CHAPTER VI.

THE HORRORS OF LIBBY PRISON—THE FOOD—THE VERMIN.

The process of plundering the men of what little effects they managed to secrete about them having been completed, we were ordered up to the third story, and packed in a room with others, making the number of occupants 270 in our apartment. We had nothing to eat, and many of us were suffering from hunger as well as fatigue. Finding we must fast till morning, we made arrangements to lie down, but this was no easy matter. We were so thickly stowed that I had not room to stretch my limbs, although the men were wedged as close as possible. Standing, sitting, or laying down, we were most uncomfortably crowded. In spite of free ventilation, the air we breathed was contaminated, and each prisoner was constantly inhaling this offensive atmosphere.

Next morning many of us were suffering all the tortures that hunger can inflict, but still no rations. Noon came without a morsel to eat, and not until 3 o'clock in the afternoon did we receive the welcome tidings that rations were to be served out. We formed ourselves into messes of twenty, and received our quota. My share consisted of a piece of corn bread one and a half inches broad and two inches long, about a tablespoonful of beans, and a piece of bacon weighing two ounces, lean, and literally covered with maggots. The stench from it was sickening. Hungry as I was I could not stomach *that*, so I eat my corn bread, which was a compound of corn, corn-cobs and hulls, all ground up together, and scarcely fit for horse feed.

Such were the rations apportioned to us for twenty-four hours, and such was our daily fare, in quality and quantity, for nine days, without any variation. Suffering from hunger, however, was not the only annoyance. The abundance of vermin scarcely permitted us to rest day or night. The building was "alive" with them—every crack and crevice filled—*working* with these disgusting insects. They lodged in our clothing, in our hair and whiskers, making a continual war upon us; and, in spite of our best efforts, they maintained the mastery. Only those who have endured the torments vermin inflict can imagine the punishment and misery they brought upon us. How often we reverted to the clean linen and snow-white bedding we had been accustomed to in our comfortable homes, and contrasted it with our present wretched condition.

Under such circumstances, the sick and wounded could hope for no comfort. Many a poor fellow could have been saved from the "dead trench" had he received even the treatment due a man in robust health; but food, medicine, and the care necessary to a sick man, were never dispensed at the "Libby." Death was often hastened by the misery incident to the horrible condition of the place, and even the most sturdy constitutions became shattered.

CHAPTER VII.

A MOVE FOR ANDERSONVILLE—INCIDENTS OF THE PASSAGE—INHUMANITY OF THE REBELS—WOMAN'S SYMPATHY.

On the 22d of June, about 3 o'clock in the morning, we were ordered to pack up, which was no very hard job, and received a scanty supply of provisions previous to leaving the scene of our misery. Soon we were on the move, and as we marched through the streets of Richmond, I felt a happy relief while breathing the pure air of heaven. All seemed delighted to make an escape from present ills, though apprehensive that we were only "jumping out of the frying pan into the fire."

We marched to the Richmond and Danville Railroad Depot, got aboard the cars, and started for Danville, on our way to that soldier's sepulchre, Andersonville Prison. Seventy of us were packed in a light baggage car, and the reader can imagine the acute suffering we endured, traveling in a box car, so closely stowed, in the month of June. At Danville we received an apology for rations, and took the train there for our destination.

We had a number of poor fellows on board who were fast sinking under these cruelties, three of whom died. Others were hanging between life and death, and had they died on the passage they would have been saved a more agonizing death. There was one invalid in our car who had been badly wounded in the hand, which was shattered in a horrible manner, and was then in process of mortification. He was fevered, and suffering all the agony incident to a neglected wound. The poor fellow's constant cry for water excited the sympathy of all in the car, but not a drop could be obtained. Indeed, there were others craving water, who would have paid any price, had they possessed the means, for sufficient to slake their intolerable thirst.

In course of time the train reached a station, where a stop was made to take in water, and I ventured to ask of the guard permission to get the sick man a drink, stating that he was very ill; but I received no answer. The man still crying for water in such piteous tones, I once more approached the guard and made another appeal.

"Guard," said I, "for God's sake let me get that poor fellow some water. He is wounded badly and cannot live long."

"Don't you know we ain't 'lowed to talk to you? What in —— are you doing here, you g—— d—— Yankee? What business you got here, anyhow?"

This was the reply; and that inhuman wretch denied me the privilege of alleviating the torture of a dying man, for he breathed his last on the train.

The first sympathy manifested for us, strange to say, was noticed in South Carolina. If I mistake not, the place was called Pleasant Mills. I was standing close to the guards, watching for an opportunity to quench my violent thirst, when I saw a young girl, very plainly attired, standing on an embankment close to the cars. I at length caught her eye, and, addressing her, begged her to dip me up some water from a small pool lying close to the road.

"Why," said she, "that is not fit to drink."

"Oh, that will do. I am nearly famished for water. Please fill my measure."

"I will get you better water than that," she said, and started toward the house. In a very short time she returned with two others, each carrying a pail of pure spring water. They soon dealt it out to us, and again went to the spring and refilled them. These noble-hearted girls kept on with their work of mercy until the cars started, when the heartfelt gratitude of the men burst out in blessings which, I trust, they have fully realized. Some of my companions had a few rings and other trifles secreted about them, and threw them to the girls. I had nothing but thanks to offer, and these I expressed in the best language I could command. Certainly, I never felt the inconvenience of poverty more than on that occasion.

The rebels, however, seemed to care but little for

the life, health or comfort of their prisoners. Indeed, we question if history presents a parallel to their brutality in any war between civilized nations. Few conflicts exhibit the same degree of intense hatred and personal ill-feeling as that which was displayed during the rebellion. At one of the stations on our route some of the men were permitted to get out to answer the necessary purposes of life, but, of course, under the eye of the guard. One old man, far beyond the legal limit of a soldier's age, and much enfeebled by the hardships he had encountered, was somewhat tardy, and when he reached the cars they were in motion. He tried to get on, but his best efforts failed, and, after clinging to the car for some time, fell off. The guard deliberately leveled his piece and fired. The old man dropped dead, and could scarcely know what killed him, as we did not see a limb or muscle move.

On a Sabbath afternoon we reached Savannah, where we laid over all night. We stopped in the suburbs of the city, and throngs of people were continually coming and going—manifesting great desire to see the "Yanks." Among the visitors was an elderly lady, accompanied by a little child—perhaps a grand-daughter—eating a piece of bread. A squad of us were standing together, inside of the guards, when they approached. One of the men asked the child for a piece of bread. She immediately threw the piece in her hand toward us. The guard, in a very rough manner, exclaimed—

"If you do that again I will arrest you."

"I don't care," replied the little lump of humanity, "if anybody is hungry I *will* give them bread when I have it."

The old lady left at once; but in about half an hour she returned with a basket. Taking a position opposite us she watched an opportunity, when she threw the basket and contents at us. It contained four loaves of bread, a quantity of cooked eggs, a lot of potatoes and a piece of bacon. The guard flew into a violent passion and raved immoderately at the old lady. She fearlessly retorted, however, and in a brogue that told us we were indebted to a warm Irish heart for the welcome food:

"An' shure, wud yez like to be starvin' yer own self, and not a piece to stay the hunger? Yez ought to be wid 'em, and have a taste of the tratement ye give 'em."

Our profuse thanks seemed to be a rich reward for the kind-hearted old lady; and the eagerness with which we clutched her precious gift, must have convinced her that it was a timely charity.

Our guards were very severe upon us, and would not permit any of the traders, at the different stopping places, to approach us. Some of these had corn bread and other articles of food for sale, which several who had secreted money about them would have purchased at any price. But I will not longer dwell upon the painful incidents connected with our passage. Let me live to what age I may, I shall never revert to them without a shudder.

I have purposely alluded to the kind offices performed by the ladies mentioned in this chapter, because of the vindictive spirit so generally manifested by Southern women against Union soldiers. The exceptions alluded to, however, were to be found in the humbler walks of life. Those of the "chivalry" standard often disgraced the sex by bestowing upon us scoffs, jeers, and applying epithets which indicated anything but refinement.

CHAPTER VIII.

ANDERSONVILLE—THE PRISON PEN—CAPTAIN WIRZ—
A SCENE OF MISERY.

We reached Andersonville about the 28th of June. We were all elated with the impression that we were going to far more comfortable quarters, since one of the guards relieved our apprehensions by stating that it was a fine plantation. Now, my idea of a plantation pictured a magnificent building, with ample shade around it, and a number of adjoining buildings, particularly adapted to our accommodation; but what was my astonishment to see in the distance a large space of ground inclosed by a stockade, without a single tree in the inclosure, surrounded by a forest as far as the eye could see.

We were marched from the station to a building overlooking the pen. Over the main entrance was a pine board, with the following announcement: "Captain Wirz, Commander of the Inner Prison." We halted before this building, where we were compelled to remain in the broiling sun for two hours, suffering intense agony from thirst; at the end of that time the notorious Wirz made his appearance, and saluted us in a broad German accent: "Fall in, you got tam Yankee s—— of b——s." He was a Swiss, however, a fact since learned during his trial.

What a disgrace to a sister Republic! What a libel upon an ancestry whose noble deeds adorn the pages of history, that such a monster should claim birthright in the land of Tell! It is to be regretted that the proud traits of a nation, which assimilates so closely to our own, and which, at one time, commanded the admiration of the world, should be so wholly lost sight of in the present century. Tyranny and treason, unfortunately, can always find hirelings in the degenerate sons of a once noble race. But I am digressing.

"Captain" Wirz formed us into detachments of 270, and divided that number into three messes of 90 each. My detachment was the 72d, and I was placed in the first mess. We were then ushered into the pen. I shall never forget the heart-sinking and utter despair which came over me when this broad scene of misery was first opened to my view. It was enough to appal the stoutest heart. We found a mass of human beings crowded together, almost a jam, with scarcely space enough to move about or lie down.

Although the pen was originally designed to hold but 10,000 men, I found about 22,000 in it. And such a collection of emaciated, squalid creatures I never beheld. Scarcely one of them wore a whole garment, none had a complete suit, the most of them could not hide their nakedness, and not a few of them were in a perfectly nude state. It would be impossible for me to represent to the reader the horrors of this scene just as I saw it. Men were crawling and creeping from sheer starvation, unable to stand erect. Others moved about with ghost-like appearance—their hollow cheeks, sunken eyes and tottering steps denoting their rapid approach to the grave or pit—for there was no Christian burial there. Wherever I turned misery stared me in the face—starvation was doing its work. And yet thousands of these victims had left comfortable homes, where they enjoyed full and plenty.

I was, for a time, completely bewildered—scarcely knowing whether I was awake or dreaming. Involuntarily I asked myself the question: "Is this hell?" *Twenty-two thousand* human beings, at one time hearty, stalwart men, now reduced to this condition by that inhuman "Commander of the Inner Prison," who was no doubt carrying out the orders of his superiors. I am unwilling to believe that the rebel authorities were cognizant of the real condition of their prison pens; but I do accuse them of giving to such monsters as Wirz unlimited license to treat the men as their passions or prejudices dictated. That such unfeeling wretches should abuse this power was to be expected.

CHAPTER IX.

INCIDENTS OF PRISON LIFE — THE CARTEL — THE "DEAD LINE."

We had scarcely entered the pen, when we were surrounded by crowds of poor fellows, anxious to learn how the war was progressing, and especially to glean some tidings of an exchange of prisoners. It was the hope, from day to day, that an exchange would be effected, which sustained many, and enabled them to live through the trials, exposure and starvation of prison life. But for this, thousands would have yielded to despair, and ceased to make an effort to preserve life.

And here let me say that, whoever was the cause of suspending the cartel, or preventing an exchange of prisoners, has a fearful account to settle. When men were dying by thousands, it was no time to cavil or stand upon a point of military etiquette. The government was not wholly ignorant of our sufferings, and could not have been humiliated by any concessions calculated to rescue these brave men from a slow and torturing death. If there is policy in war, there is also policy in mercy, whether dispensed according to discipline or not; and it is due to the brave men who endured all the horrors of

Southern prisons, that the nation they so nobly
served, should place itself above suspicion in a
matter which entailed so much of death and misery
upon our gallant soldiers.

I fortunately met with a member of the regiment
to which I belonged, and he secured me a place to lie
down. I needed rest, and it was a most gracious
relief, even there, as I was weary and nearly exhausted. My comrade gave me a detailed account
of the rules and regulations which governed the
inclosure, and called my special attention to a little
rail-line, some twenty feet from the stockade. "As
you value your life," said he, "do not step between
that and the stockade. *It is the dead line.*" He
also cautioned me against a gang of raiders, composed of our own men, who would rob and murder a
man for ten cents.

I soon realized the value of this last caution. A
companion of mine who had entered the pen with
me, having no place to sleep, was compelled to lay
down with some others on the only space left for a
wagon road. He had not lain there long, when he
was seized by the hair of the head and a knife held
to his throat, while a fellow soldier rifled his pockets
of the little money he possessed. A number of such
cases occurred, and so frequent became these outrages, that it was found necessary to adopt prompt
and severe measures to check the evil. Accordingly,
six offenders, who had just participated in a very

aggravated assault and robbery, were apprehended by ourown men. They were tried in the most impartial manner under the circumstances, condemned, and sentenced to be hung. This sentence was carried into effect on the 11th day of July, 1864. After that we had comparative peace, and felt more secure. At least, no more murders were committed, and few, if any, robberies.

I know that some may pronounce this a summary proceeding; but I consider that the necessities arising from our peculiar situation demanded it. Some 22,000 men were there huddled together—victims of every species of privation, and driven to despair. With phrensied minds and craving appetites, every latent feeling of selfishness was awakened into activity. Conscience was blunted by suffering, and the love of life destroyed all scruples in regard to the means of preserving it. In this condition, it is not surprising that they should prey upon one another. And yet, it was absolutely necessary to check such lawlessness as the only means of protecting the weak against the strong; and where so many were packed, it was apparent that all must suffer, unless the most rigid discipline was maintained, and the evil-disposed restrained by proper punishment.

In the meantime, an addition to the stockade was in course of construction. When that was completed, my detachment, with a number of others, were removed to the new inclosure. Our rations were dealt out here rather more liberally than in Libby Prison, but in quality about the same. They grew less, however, week after week, until they came down to the Libby measure.

I would, were it possible, describe some of the horrors of this pen of death; but I confess myself inadequate to the task. Neither my powers of description, nor my command of language, can do the subject justice. My best efforts can only give a vague idea of the reality.

It is proper to state that I had charge of the sick of my mess, comprising ninety men. When there was a doctor's call, I took such of the sick out as were able to walk, and those entirely disabled I had placed upon stretchers. It was on such occasions that I could see, in a clear light, the suffering and slow murder of the men. The most of them were mere frames—a batch of bones hung together like skeletons in a medical college,—but exhibiting sufficient animation to give them, if possible, a more ghostly appearance.

Many of these poor fellows were afflicted with offensive sores. Different portions of the body and limbs were eaten out, and maggots were working thick in the cavities. In some cases gangrene set in, and mortification followed. There were no means at hand to wash and cleanse the parts thus affected, and men were wasting away and dying in the most loathsome condition. Groans and shrieks, curses and prayers, the ravings of delirium, and agonizing cries, mingled in one confused chorus, and served to drown the murmurs of those less boisterous in their complaints.

At first I thought it impossible to exist in the midst of such horrors; but I soon became familiarized with the misery around me, and learned to look upon those suffering most acutely with almost stoical indifference. Nothing more than such scenes is better calculated to deaden and render inactive the refined sensibilities of our nature. The soldier learns to look upon carnage unmoved, the surgeon amputates with more concern for his professional reputation than sympathy for his patients, and a nurse, in this den of woe, performs his duties mechanically, with but little exhibition of feeling for those in his care. I do not claim to be an exception wholly; but, while I strived to do all I could for the sick in my charge, I soon overcame the feelings of depression awakened when I first assumed the position. Then, it must be remembered, that we looked upon the sick and dying as only a step in advance of us, and that we must soon travel the same road to our long home. But while thus apparently insensible to all emotion, every act of kindness that could alleviate pain, or render the sick more comfortable, was cheerfully performed.

In this connection, I feel it a duty to allude to the kind and humane feelings manifested by Drs. Rice, Bates and Holmes. Dr. Rice, especially, is entitled to my warmest thanks for words of cheer and professional advice. This was all he could give, as he had no means of obtaining medicine for us, and would not be permitted to administer it if he had. But his was a sympathizing heart, and he encouraged and gave hope to the desponding. The three gentlemen named will long be remembered with gratitude by those who survived the perils of that prison-pen. Truly, "kind words never die."

As sergeant of the sick of our mess, I had all the most hopeless cases to attend to. Disease and misery, in all its forms, was constantly before me, and few men, in the same space of time, ever witnessed more of human suffering. One unfortunate invalid, Wm. Thompson, a member of the Third Massachusetts Regiment, was an object of my especial sympathy. He was daily wasting away, and was conscious that he could not survive many days. He grew despondent, then indifferent, and apparently patiently awaited the summons of the grim messenger. Too soon, however, he manifested certain indications of insanity. He would sit or lie in one place day after day, unless removed. "Oh, sergeant, can you do nothing for me?" was the question he constantly propounded. I could only furnish him with water, and give him such words of encouragement as occurred to my mind. I obtained no information from him in regard to his family, except that his parents resided in Massachusetts. He soon became a passive, quiet idiot, and talked occasionally about his father and mother, but so incoherently that I could glean nothing definite. The poor fellow lingered about two weeks after he became delirious before he died. Like many others, he was literally covered with vermin. I was much interested in Thompson, and sought every opportunity to get some intelligent statement from him, that I might transmit it to "the loved ones at home," but in vain.

To give some idea of our filthy surroundings, I will state that a small brook coursed through the stockade, and a cook-house stood near it. The encampment of the rebel guards bordered on this little stream, outside of the pen. All the offal and refuse of the cook-house, and, more disgusting still, the filth and excrement, daily deposited, was carried off by this small run of water. Yet, for some time after I arrived, we were compelled to drink, cook and wash with it. In fact, it was used for all purposes, until wells were subsequently excavated.

Inside of the stockade there was about six acres of swamp; that was used as a common sink by 40,000 men, for the pen was now greatly enlarged. The quality of the water may be estimated when the reader is informed that every offensive substance, accumulating from this large number of men, was drained into the stream, from which we had to use it for all purposes. In order to obtain a dipper of water more pure, some of them would reach over the "dead line" in search of a clearer spot in the brook. But such rashness seldom failed to bring the punishment of death.

As I approached the stream one morning, I saw a poor creature staggering on ahead of me, with nothing on him but the remnant of an old shirt. The swamp was very soft and miry, and any person stepping off the plank would mire in it. It was loathsome and offensive in the extreme. Suddenly I heard the report of a gun. I saw the poor fellow reel, totter and fall. He was pierced through his entire body with a rifle ball. Being weak and feeble, he was in danger of falling off the plank, and came so near it once that he incautiously leaned on the "dead line" for support until he recovered himself. This is the crime for which he was shot down like a dog.

In the stream alluded to, those who were able washed their persons. On one occasion, after I had gone through this process, I saw a member of the Twelfth Pennsylvania Cavalry shot through the breast while in the act of reaching over the "dead line" for his shirt. He had accidentally dropped it over, and in his efforts to regain it was instantly shot down.

I came very near paying the same penalty for my rashness in unnecessarily exposing myself. The rebels were doing some repairs on the stockade, and were chopping down some trees for that purpose. The chips were flying around in various directions between the stockade and the "dead line," and I incautiously stooped to pick one up. Casting my eyes toward the guard, I saw him cover me with his rifle. I was too quick for him, however, so I lost my chip and he his furlough; for it was generally understood, that for every Yankee shot, his murderer received thirty days' furlough. While I cannot vouch for the truth of this, I do know that the guard was invariably relieved after shooting a prisoner.

And here it may be proper to give a description of the stockade. It consisted of very large pine trees, about twenty-six feet high, set perpendicular in the ground about six feet deep, and placed closely together. About twenty feet from the stockade was a small rail or post fence about three feet high. This was the celebrated dead line. It was covered over on the top, making a shelter for the guards, who were stationed about thirty yards apart.

My anxiety to obtain the chips, was occasioned by the scarcity of fuel to cook the miserable and scant food furnished us. We were allowed two large sticks of cord-wood, which we cut up in small pieces, as that quantity had to last three days for ninety men. This stinted supply was the more aggravating, because wood was abundant in the vicinity. Dense forests surrounded the inclosure, and yet we were denied enough to cook "corn dodgers," (a term given to a mixture of coarse corn meal and water.) We were in the condition of the shipwrecked mariner, clinging to a plank, with water all around him, but could not use it.

It was evident that the leading rebels deliberately fixed upon plans to exterminate, to a certain extent, their prisoners; and I have always believed that this work of death was planned in Richmond, and carried out by that abominable butcher — Wirz. Hunger and thirst were the two great agencies to be used; and these, added to nakedness and exposure, did their work most effectually.

Our rations mostly consisted of one pint of Indian meal per day. This was ground very nearly as coarse as hominy, with the cob, hulls and all ground up together. I undertook, on several occasions, to separate the hulls and the cobs from the meal, but I found it made my allowance so small that I desisted, and only culled out the large pieces of the cob. To the pint of corn meal was added two ounces of bacon, two spoonsful of beans, and about as much salt as you could hold on the handle of a spoon. That was to sustain life for twenty-four hours. The quality of the bacon was often such as to sicken those who looked upon it; yet, we were glad to get it. Think of it! And then reflect that, with this scanty subsistence, 40,000 men were huddled together in a pen, packed so close that we had scarcely room for rollcall. But enough of this pen of horrors. I left 14,000—800 of them my comrades—in the cold embrace of death, their bones reposing in ditches or trenches, thrown together as though they were of the brute creation.

I could cite numerous instances of this kind, but the details are too sickening, and would only pain me to rehearse them, while they could afford no pleasure to the reader. It is as lamentable as true, however, that a number who had abandoned all hope of deliverance, borne down by disease and starvation, deliberately stepped over the "dead line," and courted death, in order to escape the torment and suffering they were enforced to endure. The shooting of men stepping one foot over that line was so common that it ceased to attract attention, or to create surprise. As soon as the report of a gun was heard, the general expression was, "another man paroled."

I now began to realize that I was in a very critical condition. My shoes had dropped from my feet perfectly worthless. I was growing weaker every day, and sometimes I thought I should sink down and die in my tracks. My pantaloons were fast wearing out, and I was compelled to cut off the legs below the knee to patch other parts, in order to cover my nakedness. I was bare-legged, bare-headed, and bare-footed; for my hat was so much worn that it was no longer a covering for my head. I obtained the tail of a regulation coat from my companion, and made three scull-caps out of it, of which I retained one, and partially remedied this difficulty. All this time we were exposed to the heat of a Southern sun in midsummer.

CHAPTER X.

THE CHANCES OF ESCAPE CONSIDERED—THE ATTEMPT MADE—A FAILURE—CAUGHT IN THE ACT.

It was about this time that I began to entertain serious thoughts of escape. I felt that I was dying by inches, and as the chances of life began to grow less, the more earnestly I yearned for wife, children, home and friends. I had left behind me four dear little boys—the oldest only seven years of age—and the thought of leaving my wife a widow, and my children orphans, was truly harrowing. I felt content to die if I could *die at home.* I would sit by the hour and revert to almost every act and word spoken by my wife. The childish pranks and prattle of my boys would come as fresh to the memory as though I had parted from them yesterday. It was a relief thus to recall the hours of domestic happiness I once enjoyed, and these reflections only made me more determined to see them once more, or die in the attempt.

I therefore set about some plan of deliverance. While these thoughts occupied my mind, I became intimate with a Tennesseean, to whom I broached the subject, and we soon found nine others who were willing to make the attempt. We frequently consulted about the best mode of operating, and finally came to the conclusion to tunnel under the stockade. Wells were being dug within the inclosure at the time, with the hope of obtaining a better supply of water. While this work was going on, we commenced operations in a little shanty our leader had erected for himself—a rare luxury, that few enjoyed, and which must have cost him a pretty handsome sum. This was in close proximity to the well-diggers, and gave us an opportunity to place our dirt, under cover of night, on the heap thrown out by the diggers. Thus secure from observation, we worked faithfully, day and night, taking turns. Our only tools consisted of an old shovel, or part of a shovel, and a haversack, in which we removed the dirt. We worked hard, and at the end of three weeks, had extended our tunnel outside of the stockade. We were buoyant—almost happy—at the bright promise before us, and each felt sanguine of success.

One morning, however, perhaps only a day before we intended to make the venture, a rebel soldier with some six negroes, entered the shanty, apparently fully apprised of our plans, although we had taken great pains to conceal everything calculated to excite suspicion. The mouth, or entrance to the tunnel, was carefully covered up every time we left it. They at once removed the covering, and the evidence of our

3*

guilt was before them. Of course, the shanty was stripped forthwith.

There we were, caught in the act. A rebel spy had betrayed us, but who, we never knew. We knew not what would be the consequences, or what would be the punishment. We consoled ourselves with the reflection, however, that they could devise none, except death, that would be more severe than the suffering we endured from day to day. But, strange to say, we heard but little of it afterward. Thus, the labor of three weeks was lost to us, and our hearts sank within us as our hopes of freedom fled.

Still, we did not abandon all thoughts of escape. About the latter part of July, they commenced the erection of a stockade about one hundred feet from the main one, so that put a stop to our tunneling. In the meantime, the mortality was increasing fearfully. Each day as high as two hundred, and sometimes two hundred and thirty, were released from their sufferings by death. The carnage of battle, the worst form of pestilence, never equalled it. Fevers, unhealed wounds, sores, gangrene, and every disease incident to heat, storm and exposure, added to starvation, kept up the sick list to a high figure. Indeed, many of them welcomed death as a friend. It was a common occurrence to wake up in the morning and find a corpse beside the living.

But, there were others who struggled hard for life. They would speak of wife, children, parents and kindred, in the most piteous tones; and it was truly distressing to see men who had faced the cannon's mouth unflinchingly, cry like children, as they felt conscious that they never would look upon their dear old homes again. For my own part, I began to grow reckless of life as the pangs of hunger increased, and I pondered upon a choice between death by starvation or death from an attempt to escape.

CHAPTER XI.

OUR REMOVAL TO FLORENCE—FALLACIOUS HOPES.

About this time, we learned that the noble Sherman began to menace Atlanta, and that General Stoneman had a force which would attempt our rescue. Too soon we lost all hope of deliverance from this expedition, as we were informed that he and his forces were captured. Again we were cheered by the news that General Sherman had captured Atlanta, and rumors of exchange went from lip to lip, inspiring new hope, and acting like electricity upon the spirits of the men. This was the burden of our song night and day. Lying down on the hard ground at night, or rising with aching limbs and hungry stomachs in the morning, we discussed the probabilities of an exchange.

Thus time passed, our condition growing from bad to worse. Our hopes alternated as one report died out and another one reached us, of a speedy exchange. Again it came; but this time in a more tangible shape,—as we received orders to move. Every heart leaped with joy, every eye sparkled with delight. Oh, it was a joyous time! The dying prayed for life, the sick and desponding revived, the weak grew stronger. All was bustle and activity.

The prisoners were taken out by detachments. I

went with the 32d. With a buoyant heart I turned my back upon that den of misery, in the full assurance from the guards that we were to be exchanged; and I already began to anticipate a happy meeting with my wife and children. We took the cars for Macon in high glee, having been first supplied with what they termed two days of rations, but not sufficient to make one hearty meal, and the quality about as before described. We laid over all night at Macon. Next morning we started on our journey, crossing the Savannah River, and soon got into South Carolina. We halted at a station, when an officer came to the guards and gave orders to permit no man to get out of the cars, and to shoot any one who made the attempt.

We arrived at Florence, after being two days and nights on the journey, with nothing to eat, save the two rations before mentioned, and nearly starved. Here we learned, to our amazement, that no exchange would take place. All our hopes were frustrated; and the reaction from the highest expectations to utter despair, left us in a most wretched condition, mentally as well as physically.

We were ushered into a pen, where we found some 5,000 of our comrades, and received some rations, which were greedily devoured. Many of us hoped that our stay at Florence would be short, and consoled ourselves with the belief that our journey to this place was but preliminary to a speedy exchange; but time served to banish this delusion.

CHAPTER XII.

ANOTHER PLAN OF ESCAPE—WE RESOLVE TO "RUN THE GUARDS"—THE FLIGHT—BLOODHOUNDS ON OUR TRACK—PERILS OF OUR SITUATION—THEY LOSE OUR TRAIL.

It would be a difficult task to picture the despair which now overwhelmed me. I could no longer cover my nakedness with the few rags on my person, and my strength was fast wasting away. What to do I did not know. I felt that if I made the attempt to escape, I must do so while I had strength for exertion. A few more days of suffering would render me helpless, and death could not long be delayed. I consulted with a friend about "running the guards;" for I saw they were building a new stockade, which would materially lessen the chances of successful flight. But that experiment was declared to be certain death.

At length I found a man named Bradley, of the 90th Illinois regiment—whom I fixed upon as a suitable companion, and one whom I could trust with the dangerous proposition. After consulting with him upon the subject, I remarked—

"Frank, I feel that I cannot live long. I am sinking fast—what plan of escape can you suggest?"

"I scarcely know," he replied; "cannot we sneak out?"

"No—impossible!"

"True—we are encircled with guards."

"Well, let us run the gauntlet."

"That is dangerous—one chance for life, three for death."

"Frank, it is certain death to go into that stockade. I say run the gauntlet—liberty or death."

"I'm in," said he—(an expression among soldiers denoting hearty assent.)

We accordingly made preparations to "make a dash," as opportunity presented. There was a double line of guards about one hundred yards from the first line. Our plan was to run before the double line was posted, which duty was generally performed about dark. It was a critical moment to both of us. We knew that the odds were decidedly against success, and that failure was certain death; but sooner than endure the misery of longer imprisonment, we resolved to make the venture.

We went to the lines and scrutinized the guards. It was arranged that a few friends, to whom our secret was confided, should also come to the lines, and scatter themselves, in order to prevent suspicion. Just about dusk, we approached the spot we had selected for a "bolt," near which we carelessly loitered for a short time, and saw the outer guards taking post. And now the terrible moment arrived.

At a given signal from my friend, we darted through the lines between the guards.

Almost simultaneously we heard the command, "Halt!" and the report of a rifle. The ball cut my old pants, or what was left of them, above the knee grazing the flesh, but drawing no blood. The outward line of guards were very near us, and fired upon us, but not a single shot took effect. Away we sped, hatless, shoeless, and nearly naked. Fear gave speed to our flight, for well we knew it was a struggle between life and death.

We made for the railroad, the track of which was in a cut some ten feet deep. This was reached in safety, and we got down the embankment with little difficulty, but I was too weak to ascend the other side, and my companion, who was much stronger, because not long a prisoner, readily assisted me up, after running along the track some distance to find a more convenient place. I was so weak that this exertion almost exhausted my strength, and had not Frank pulled me up, I must have been captured.

We entered a cornfield on a run, and when about the centre of it, Frank paused to look back. I heard him exclaim, "My God, they are after us!" I gave a hurried glance backward, and could see the outline of a squad of pursuers hurrying over the fence. We both dropped to the earth, and lay in a prostrate position in a furrow. While hiding ourselves as best we could, we heard them tramping all

around us, and expected every moment to see a muzzle pointed toward us. We thought our time had come. In a few minutes I heard one of them interrogate another—
"Which way have they gone?"
"They must have passed this spot, or very near it," was the reply.

They could not have been ten yards from us when this conversation was going on. However, they passed us, and went off in a northerly direction. About this time, when the sound of their footsteps had scarcely died in the distance, we heard the bay of bloodhounds, and knew they were upon the track. Oh, what a terrifying sound to fleeing fugitives! Quick as thought I pictured to myself a most horrible death, and expected to be torn in pieces by those ravenous brutes; for I am told they are allowed but scanty food in order to make them more desperate in pursuit. Rather would I have heard the report of rifles than the dreadful warning sent out by these savage dogs. I involuntarily exclaimed, "Heaven help us, Frank; it is life or death now."

We ran to the cover of what seemed to be a large forest, in front of us, but it proved to be a dense swamp,—my companion passing me a little to the left. As soon as possible, I ascended a tree for safety, and, although apparently secure from immediate attack, still my heart sank within me, as I heard the bloodhound bay growing more and more distinct, and rapidly nearing me; for I knew if they once laid eyes on me, they would hold me where I was until the guard came up.

I cannot describe my feelings, as I clung to a projecting limb, awaiting my doom. There I was, a poor, starved fugitive, a moving skeleton, weak and exhausted, some fifteen bloodhounds upon my trail, and a horrible death awaiting me, if able to reach my person,—or death by a bullet, if caught by the guards. It was to me a period of rapid thought, in which my wife and children, and their helpless condition, rose up before me in life-like colors. My dangerous situation brought out all my affectionate concern for those dear to me; and I felt it was hard to die *such* a death while making a last effort to embrace them once more.

But God, in his mercy, came to my help. Still holding on to the tree, and almost overcome with terror, I began to feel sure that the hounds had taken another direction, as the sound of their baying seemed to gradually recede. Soon, to my great joy, it became more indistinct, and I concluded they must have been thrown off my trail where I had waded through some water, and had followed that of the rebel guards.

I returned thanks to Almighty God for my deliverance, and descended from the tree to search for my friend. This I did most thoroughly for some time, but without success. This misfortune was another erious blow to my prospects of escape; for I felt very dependent upon Frank, from the fact that he had served with General Sherman, and would prove a valuable pilot, as we had previously arranged to strike for Tennessee. I confess his loss made me feel very despondent, aside from my deep concern for his safety. I knew not then, nor do I know now, whether he reached home and friends, or was butchered in cold blood by the pursuing guards. Sometimes the possibility of his being torn in pieces by the bloodhounds occurred to me; but sincerely do I hope that he escaped all peril by flood or field, bloodhounds or rebel guards.

CHAPTER XIII.

LIFE IN FOREST AND SWAMP—PRECARIOUS SUBSISTENCE—HELP FROM AN UNEXPECTED SOURCE.

Although thankful for my escape so far, I was oppressed by the worst apprehensions. I was quite ignorant of the country, without a compass, surrounded by enemies, alone in a dense swamp, my strength gone, possessing no facilities for cooking—even if I obtained food,—a thousand miles from home, and in a State where neither mercy or charity could be expected by a "man wearing the blue."

I put my trust in God, to whom I appealed for aid, and struck out with all the resolution I could muster—taking the North star as my guide. I walked on until I reached a rice swamp, and soon after leaving that, found a sweet potatoe field, where I dug out a few and devoured them greedily. On—on I traveled, making every effort to leave as wide a distance as possible between my late quarters and myself.

I traveled all that night faithfully, through swamps, woods, and sugar-cane fields, buoyed up by hope, rejoicing that the bloodhounds were no longer upon my track. About daybreak I discovered a house in the distance, but deemed it prudent to give it a wide berth. I visited a neighboring cornfield, however, and gathered some corn, when I again took to the forest, and sought the most dense part of it, where I made a bed of leaves, eat some of the grain with great difficulty, laid down and slept all day, weary and fatigued, till toward evening.

When I awoke, my limbs pained me very much. This was, no doubt, caused by over-exertion and general prostration. After dark, I again started on my journey, still looking to the North star as my guide. I traveled all that night, trying to subsist on corn, but my teeth had become loose, and my gums so very sore with scurvy, that I was unable to masticate it. I very much feared that if I could procure no substitute for corn, I should die of starvation. I then tried beans, which are cultivated quite as extensively at the South as corn. They are called peas by the inhabitants, and constitute an essential article of food in that section; but I found but little nutriment in them in their natural state. My sufferings from hunger soon became intolerable, and I felt myself growing weaker every hour. I kept to the woods, however,—eating berries and whatever I could find as a substitute for food.

On the third day, I found myself in the vicinity of a plantation, and endeavored to have an interview with some of the negroes. For this purpose I loitered about the place all day, but had no opportunity to communicate with any of them. While here, I found some grapes, which were not only palatable, but proved an excellent remedy for my sore gums. Footsore and weary, I once more resumed my journey after dark, and went on until I came to a magnificent pine forest. That night I suffered intense agony from hunger, and became so weak that I staggered like a drunken man.

In all my travels that day, I had seen no signs of a human habitation—nothing that gave me any hope of procuring food. In my despair, I exclaimed aloud, "My God, shall I die of starvation in this forest?" Hunger seemed to overcome every other feeling, and I ceased to fear the consequences of a capture. I almost felt as if I could hail the rebel guards had they been in sight. Oh, what a long night!—what an endless forest! Day dawned, and found me still in it, tottering along with unsteady step until after sunrise, when I laid down by a tree.

My feet and legs were badly scratched, bleeding and smarting with pain. My old clothes were in rags—torn almost in shreds by the underbrush—retaining barely sufficient to hide my nakedness.

Altogether, I was a most emaciated, miserable-looking being.

I had not rested more than fifteen minutes, however, before I heard a very singular noise, similar to the screech of a peacock. I started up, at first supposing that it proceeded from some wild animal.

After listening a short time, I came to the conclusion that it was a human voice, and resolved to satisfy myself upon that point. Proceeding in the direction of the sound for about half a mile, I saw something like a dwelling, in a clearing, but it presented a very dilapidated appearance. I slowly approached, and saw a man in a corn-crib. He would occasionally hollow at the top of his voice, making the noise before described, which is the usual manner down South of calling hogs in from the woods for the purpose of feeding them.

As his back was toward me, I came quite near to him before he saw me. In a short time, however, he turned, and stared at me with a surprised look; for, I confess, I presented a very wretched appearance; and, but for my wasted form and sad expression of countenance, I might have faithfully represented a strolling vagabond. He was a fine, noble looking man, about thirty years of age, rather indicating intelligence and dignity above his surroundings. I thought—and the wish may have been father to the thought—that his countenance manifested merciful instincts. I saluted him with—

"Good morning, sir."

He quickly jumped from the corn-crib, and took a seat upon the fence against which I was leaning. His reply was—

"A Yank, eh?"

"Yes, sir."

"Where did you come from?"

"Florence, sir."

"Any person with you?"

"No, sir."

"How long have you been out of prison?"

"This is the morning of the fourth day, sir?"

"What have you lived on?"

"Principally on corn and peas?"

"What! three days on corn and peas?"

"Yes, sir,—and a few berries."

"You must be hungry?"

"I am nearly starved to death. Are you a soldier?"

"Yes;"—and rolling up his shirt sleeve, he exhibited a bad wound. "I served three years with Beauregard."

"Then your term of service must be nearly out."

"No; our term of service is never out while the war continues."

He then uttered the most violent invectives against Jeff. Davis, President Lincoln, and the negroes, closing with the remark, that "this was a rich man's war and a poor man's fight."

In the meantime, his wife came out, and, surveying me from head to foot, as if determined to gratify her curiosity, addressed me in a very gentle tone of voice—

"Is you what they calls a Yankee?"

"Yes, madam." Then followed several questions

similar to those asked by the husband, which were answered as before; but she continued—

"Did they shoot at you?"

"Yes, madam;" and I exhibited the slight bruise on my leg, and the hole in the leg of my ragged pantaloons. The husband then asked—

"Where are you going?"

"I do not know. I am trying to get inside of our lines. If I could do so, I should soon reach home."

"What route do you intend taking to reach them?"

"I am really at loss, sir; for I know of none that would lead me to our army or my home."

His companion then asked—

"Have you a wife?"

"Yes, madam,—and four children."

"I would go home to them, if I could."

"I am now making an effort to do so, madam."

The husband inquired—"Did they give you anything like enough to eat in prison?"

"No, sir." I then described our rations to him. They consulted together a few moments, when the wife informed me that she would get me some breakfast.

"Oh, what joyous news to a starving man! A breakfast was something I had been a stranger to for nearly six months, and I know I looked the gratitude I could not utter, for I felt it. She entered the house—a very humble log cabin, evidently uncom-

4

fortable compared to our Northern homes, and containing a very meagre supply of furniture, among which a loom, bedstead, table, and a few chairs, were the prominent articles. In the interval, the husband asked me many questions, all of which I answered frankly, and without hesitation.

I was still uncertain what would be my fate after this meeting. I thought, from his studious and abstracted manner at times, that he was debating within himself what disposition to make of me; whether to return me to prison, or to suffer me to go on my way. I was encouraged, however, by his severe strictures upon the war, and the kindness of his wife, whose countenance betrayed a true womanly sympathy. But, I had suffered so much, that I was comparatively indifferent to my fate.

Breakfast was soon announced, and I was invited to partake in that hearty, hospitable manner peculiar to the Southern people. The meal consisted of what we call, in the Southern States, Maryland biscuit—a most excellent cake—bacon and Confederate coffee, sweetened with sorghum molasses. "Help yourself," came with hearty good meaning from both of them; but I was too ravenous to need pressing. I need not say how luscious, how gracious, the food was to me. The more I eat, the more my appetite seemed to crave; and although I knew it was dangerous, after long abstinence from food, to indulge so freely, it seemed as though I could not restrain my appetite.

The lady of the house sat opposite to me with a very interesting child in her arms; and I could see by the expression of her countenance that she was deeply affected. I ate until I paused from a sense of shame, observing which, she promptly said—

"Eat,—help yourself,—I don't care if you eat everything on the table. Oh! what would your poor wife say, to see you in this condition!" and then gave vent to her feelings in a flood of tears—crying as though her heart was overburdened with grief.

I was overwhelmed, and could only remain silent during this outburst of kind sympathy; for had I attempted to speak, I should have cried like a child. As it was, tears of sincere gratitude rolled down my cheeks. May God's choicest blessings abide with that humble but noble-hearted family. After the meal was finished, and when she became more composed, I returned thanks—(it was all I could do)—to both of them in the best language I could use, and no words ever came with more sincerity from human heart.

CHAPTER XIV.

AGAIN ON THE TRAMP—A RUSE—ANOTHER PERIOD OF SUFFERING AND PRIVATION.

When I arose from the table I could scarcely stand. I had overdone the thing—eaten too much; but to me it had been a feast—a banquet,—such as the surfeited epicure never enjoyed at the Continental or Astor. Although the coffee was made of burnt corn meal, it tasted sweeter than the best Java. I now joined the husband, with the hope of ascertaining how he would dispose of me. He broached the subject by again asking me—

"Which way are you going?"

"I scarcely know, sir. It is my desire to reach Newbern, North Carolina. I think that is the nearest point toward our lines."

"Very true; but Newbern is two hundred miles from here."

"I should not care about the distance, were it not for the danger of being taken prisoner again."

"Your best route is by the way of Cheraw. When there, get some negro to set you across the Pee Dee River, and when you get into North Carolina, you will find plenty of friends."

Oh, what a relief this was to me. Had I possessed

a fortune, I could have laid it at his feet for this assurance of his friendship. I knew he could readily send me back to prison; and although he had manifested kindness and sympathy for me, yet he might estimate his duty to the Confederacy paramount to every other feeling. And now I knew how much my suspicions had wronged my generous-hearted friend. He laid me under further obligations, by saying—"I wish I had some clothes to give you, but these I am now wearing are all I possess."

And this from a rebel soldier, in the very hot-bed of secession! Such language—such kindness—was the more welcome, because entirely unexpected. The good wife now joined us, and my benefactor continued—

"I will now hitch up my old horse to the buggy, and put you on the direct road; but I do not want to get into trouble with any person I meet. I shall give such to understand that I am taking you to jail at Darlington Court House, some eighteen miles distant. I cannot avoid passing two plantations on the route, and must resort to this ruse in order to divert suspicion.

In the meantime, his good wife—God bless her!— had provided a lot of biscuit for me, and apologised for what she considered dry eating, by saying they had consumed the last particle of meat at the morning meal. Those acquainted with Southern character, know how reluctant they are to admit poverty, and what extraordinary efforts they put forth to keep up appearances; but the impoverishments of war had wofully humbled the pride of the people. Thousands who had lived luxuriously, were glad to obtain the coarsest food, and many of them found it difficult to secure sufficient of that. The march of the rebel army scattered desolation in its track—leaving but little choice to the inhabitants, during the latter part of the struggle, between a visit from their own and the Union troops. Material for male and female apparel had also become very scarce, and the ladies, especially, found it no easy task to make a presentable appearance. I might devote a chapter to the melancholy, and often ludicrous, effects of war in this particular, which so severely taxed their ingenuity to conceal the general destitution; but it is only necessary to state, that scenes of humiliation and mortification, from such causes, were of daily occurrence in almost every locality.

After bidding the lady an affectionate farewell, and again repeating my thanks, we got into the carriage and drove off, cheered by a hearty God-speed from that warm-hearted woman.

We followed a narrow road through the woods for some time, and then came out to a fine road for that section of country. We pursued this road, until we came in sight of a house, to which my friend drove up, and commenced acting his part by calling to the inmates, in a loud voice—"Hello! Did you ever see a live Yankee?" A very portly man came out and stood upon the portico, followed by a number of women and children. There were three of the former, and they inspected me very closely—manifesting all the curiosity that could be awakened by the exhibition of some wild animal.

"Where did you find him?" inquired the planter.

"He came to my house this morning, nearly starved?"

"Why, d——n it, they suffer as bad as we do. Where are you taking him to?"

"To Darlington Court House."

"Well,—you'd better hurry up."

"Have you a revolver?" asked my friend.

"No. A revolver! Why that poor devil don't look as if he could get away from anybody."

"Oh, you don't know these Yanks as well as I do. They are slippery fellows."

The women and children hung around us until we started, apparently much gratified at the sight of "a live Yank."

We started on our journey, and traveled until we came to the next plantation, where my companion practiced the same deception. We went through a similar inspection, and answered pretty much the same questions. My friend asked for a revolver as before, with a like result, and passed on.

As we approached the place of parting, he said —"I will soon put you upon a road that leads to

Cheraw, direct. As I before remarked, get some negroes to set you across the Pee Dee, and after that you will find many who will sympathize with and assist you. Leave this stick and old rag in the wagon (a stick I used in traveling, and a wash-rag I kept to cleanse my person,) as I shall give them to understand you jumped out and ran away."

He drove on about four miles further, and put me on the right road. I grasped his hand with the most lively gratitude, and poured forth my thanks; after which I once more turned my face toward the home I yearned to reach.

When I first concluded to publish my narrative, I resolved to conceal the name of my benefactor, for fear of bringing persecution upon him; but, as time progressed, rapid changes took place in the sentiments of the Southern people. They are now, with comparatively few exceptions, disposed to "accept the situation," however reluctantly, and are sufficiently tempered by adversity to tolerate, if not approve, what they would have condemned with great severity at that time; and, if otherwise, the means of protection to loyal men are so ample, that he can scarcely be made to suffer for his kindness. Aside from this, I am unwilling that he should lose the credit of an act which ought to command the respect and admiration of every lover of the Union.

His name is MORDECAI OUTLAW; and, however uncouth it may sound, it is one that will ever be dear to me, while it will be warmly cherished by my wife and children during life. I hope and trust that the government authorities may be directed toward this man, should they need a person for any responsible position in that locality. Although he fought against us, I *know* that his heart never sanctioned the treason, and that the defeat of the rebels was not a "lost cause" to him. Like thousands of others, he was irresistibly borne along by the current of rebellion, when any attempt to stem it would have brought upon him scorn and persecution, if not death.

I once more found myself in a wilderness, nearly a thousand miles from home, in the midst of an enemy's country. However, hope gave me a stout heart, and, to use a soldier's phrase, I resolved to "trust to luck, and stare fate in the face." I penetrated a large swamp, but walked in great misery, which was caused by my greedy breakfast. I had suffered much all day, and began to fear an attack of fever. In such an event, I knew I must die far from human sight, as the prostrate condition of my system could offer but a feeble resistance to disease. Fortunately, as my food digested, I grew better.

When evening came, I struck out, flanked a large farm house, and entered an extensive pine forest. When I had traveled about two hours, I became very thirsty, but could find no water. Every moment added to my suffering, until my mouth and throat became dry and parched, and my tongue began to swell. None but those who have been similarly situated can form an idea of the intense agony extreme thirst will produce. I searched in vain for any indications of water, but could see nothing to give me hope. I chewed leaves and grass in order to produce a moisture in my mouth, but they failed to give me any relief.

After reaching quite a high eminence, I descended upon the other side; and, traveling some distance, I suddenly stepped into a little brook, with a clear, gravelly bottom, which passed directly across the road. I dropped upon my knees and devoutly thanked God. After carefully washing my mouth, face and hands, I sipped the water gradually, and sat down on a log, with my feet in the brook. I took a good rest, indulging in light draughts of water until my thirst was slaked.

While sitting here, I pondered over my trials, and debated the chances of a successful termination of my efforts to escape. I often felt as now—hopeless and dispirited; but I would recall the likeness of the dear ones at home, and picture the happy meeting with them, and again my whole purpose in life would centre into an ardent desire to sit once more at my fireside, with my wife and children around me. These reflections, however, I cast aside with no little effort, and once more placed my mind upon the task before me.

I left the brook, and traveled on until daylight, reaching an open country, which I soon abandoned for the woods, where I again made a bed of leaves, eat a few biscuit, and slept well for several hours. I awoke long before night, but was afraid to move till dark. As the shadow of night came upon me, I pursued my journey, and faithfully kept upon the road to Cheraw. That night I passed four houses, all of which I successfully flanked, and, finally, entered an immense belt of woods—the most magnificent pine forest my eyes ever beheld.

And now another trouble came upon me. My feet and legs began to swell and pain me, which sadly impeded my progress, and my biscuit were all gone. I began to feel very bad, and feared I was in the incipiency of some malignant fever peculiar to that section of country. Still, I kept on, and had not proceeded far in the forest when I discovered a light ahead. The trees were so thick and tall that I could scarcely see my way, but soon discovered that the light came from a house on the road, in a clearing, just beyond.

I directed my course toward it, and had not proceeded more than ten yards, before I came upon a dark object, made partly visible by the light ahead. When nearly upon it, the growl of a bear startled me,—for a bear it was, quietly sitting upon his haunches. I was nearly overcome with terror, and expected to find myself in his embrace every moment.

But the animal did not follow me; and I looked upon my safety as another kind interposition of Providence, for which I returned devout thanks.

I followed the road till daylight, and again began to feel the torture of both hunger and thirst. Discovering a large cypress swamp ahead, I left the road and entered it. Here I fortunately found water, which afforded me partial relief. After refreshing myself, I turned to come out, but soon found the water deepening as I progressed—first reaching over my ankles, then up to my knees. I stood still for a few moments and tried to collect my thoughts. A feeling of dread came over me, and I felt bewildered. I very much feared that alligators infested these swamps, and endeavored to make my way out as soon as possible; but, in doing so, turned the wrong way,—the very reverse of that I should have gone—and came out on the road again. I laid down close by a log, and, although suffering for the want of food, slept soundly.

Oh, I shall never forget the sweet dream of home I had that day, and the gloomy awakening which told me "'twas but a dream." I thought I was sitting at my own fireside, my wife in cheerful mood, and my children romping and prattling around me. She was preparing the table for the evening meal, and soon had everything upon it that could tempt the appetite—especially shortcake, for which I have a great fondness. I could see everything just as they were when I left. It was a most natural dream—superinduced, no doubt, by the hunger I so keenly felt when I laid down. Alas—cruel disappointment! I awoke, just as I was about to take my seat at the table, to find it raining, and what few clothes I had on completely saturated.

CHAPTER XV.

A FRIENDLY NEGRO—UNEXPECTED MEETING WITH A PLANTER—ANOTHER TIMELY REFUGE.

I soon found that I was in the vicinity of a settlement. Three persons passed me during the day—one white and two colored; but I was afraid to ask for help, although in great pain. My feet were torn, swollen and bleeding, and hunger increasing. About dark I prepared to resume my journey, when I thought I could see the outline of a man through the dim twilight. He was coming toward me, and I watched his approach with great anxiety. As he came nearer, I discovered to my great joy that he was a negro. I made some trifling noise to attract his attention, when he came to a halt and looked toward me in astonishment. He stood perfectly still, in evident fear, as I approached him, and tremulously asked—

"Whoo-oo dah—who dat—who is you?"

"I am a runaway Yankee."

"Oh, de lor' bless you; you is from Florence?"

"Yes—I have recently left."

"Dey is starvin' you dah—ain't dey, honey?"

"Yes—you may well say that."

"Hab you nuthin' to eat, 'tall?"

"No—nothing."

"Well—I's got some broken pieces ob corn bread, an' a little meat yet; you wants 'em wus 'an I do—take 'em. De Lord tell me to keep dis yer bread an' meat in yer, sure."

I eagerly accepted his food, and devoured it greedily. The darkey informed me that there were no able-bodied men in the country. They had all "gone to war." I was about to bid him farewell, when he asked me where I was going. I told him I was on my way to Cheraw. "Why de lor' bless you," he exclaimed, "you is gwine right straight back to Florence." He set me right, bid me a Godspeed, and I started onward, traveling all night.

Before morning, however, my sense of sight began to fail me. I could not always see the road, and ran up against trees and bushes so frequently that my face became almost disfigured. I laid not far from a house all that day, and resumed my journey at night, although I felt myself growing weaker, and my feet and legs were now lacerated and swollen beyond description. I ceased to feel that keen sense of hunger which had so distressed me. This alarmed me, and convinced me that I could not hold out much longer. I was fast losing my vitality,—staggering as I did before reaching Mr. Outlaw's hospitable dwelling,—and should have surrendered to my fate, if the thoughts of my family had not nerved me to perseverance and greater exertion. Rousing all my energies, I went on until I could scarcely stand upon my feet. But I could not hold out, and was compelled to lie down in the night. I slept until after sunrise, got on my feet again, and slowly progressed through the forest. I was forced to stop, however, from sheer exhaustion, and rested until evening. That night I put forth every effort to proceed, although I could scarcely drag one foot after another. To add to my wretched condition, a drizzliug rain set in. I tottered along, scarcely knowing where I was going, with a growing feeling of indifference to my fate, as the chances of escape became more improbable. I had reached an uneven, gravelly country, which rendered walking very difficult, and I finally sank to the ground perfectly exhausted, exposed to the rain. While laying there, I raised myself partly to a sitting posture, and looked around for some kind of shelter. Observing a large fallen tree in a hollow not far distant, I managed to drag myself to it with great difficulty, and scraped some leaves together, where I laid down to die, as I believed, in a forest, very distant, for all I knew, from any human habitation. Here, I thought, was to be my end, after seven days and nights of wandering, save what time I slept, subsisting on but two meals, and such articles as I picked up on the way.

I laid under the tree, and being partly sheltered, soon fell asleep. I must have slept about two hours, when I was aroused by the barking of a dog. I raised up in terror, impressed with the belief that the bloodhounds were after me. As I partly raised and rested my head on my hand, I saw a dog close to the log, and several of them passed near it. I thanked God when I recognized them as the common cur. In a few moments I saw a man on horseback, approaching me from a hill a short distance off, as if following the dogs. I had placed some loose bark against the tree to shield me from the rain, and, as he neared me, I threw it aside on purpose to attract his attention. He looked toward me, and appeared to be quite startled. I at once accosted him, and said—

"Good-morning, sir."

"What in the name of heaven are you, or where did you come from?" he exclaimed.

"I am a runaway Yankee, sir."

"But where did you come from?"

"From Florence."

"How long have you been out?"

"This is the eighth day, sir."

"Where are you going?"

"I am trying to reach home."

"Where do you live?"

"In the State of New Jersey."

"How have you lived since you have been out?"

"Mostly on corn and peas, sir."

"Corn and peas!" he exclaimed, in astonishment.

"Get up and come home with me."

With great difficulty I dragged myself from the bed of leaves and got upon my feet; but they were so very painful, and all my limbs were so very stiff, that I could scarcely drag one foot after another.

"Why," said he, "you cannot walk. Are you hungry?"

"I do not feel hungry now, sir."

"When did you eat anything?"

"I have not eaten anything but peas and fox grapes for three days."

"Oh, that is awful. Get on my horse."

He alighted, partly lifted me on the log, from which I could the more readily be placed upon the horse, and walked beside me nearly a mile distant, although quite an old man. We soon approached a little house in the woods, and was met at the door by an old lady. I was left sitting on the horse while the old folks conferred together a few moments. The old gentleman then helped me to alight, and assisted me into the house. The old lady handed me a chair, and gave me words of welcome, quite in harmony with her benevolent and sympathetic expression of countenance. She propounded nearly the same questions asked by her husband, and received similar replies. Sighing audibly, she asked—

"Have you a wife?"

"Yes, madam; and four children—from whom I have not heard in the last six months."

"Oh," she exclaimed, "I wish this cruel war was

over. Don't you want to lay down, or will you have something to eat first?"

I thanked her, and said, "I would rather have a wash before eating or sleeping."

The old gentleman procured a tub, filled it with water, and placed it in a little outhouse. He led me to it, when I removed the wretched rags I wore, and commenced that refreshing process to a tired man. I was a most pitiable looking object—a mere bunch of bones—those of my hips looking as if they would protrude through the skin. Before I finished, the old gentleman came out with a shirt, a pair of drawers, and a pair of pantaloons. After a good washing, I put on the clothes, and felt like a new man. "Well," remarked my friend, "you are the poorest creature I ever did see." The word "poor" is invariably applied by Southern people to persons of wasted forms, or scarcity of flesh. "Right smart" is used to express convalescence, or general good health.

CHAPTER XVI.

A SEVERE ATTACK OF FEVER—DELIRIUM—MY HOST'S OPINION OF THE WAR—HOW IT WAS FORCED UPON THE PEOPLE.

When I resumed my chair in the house, I felt an unnatural heat coming over me, which soon pervaded my whole system. After thanking them most heartily for the clean clothes they furnished me, I requested the old lady to let me lay down. She took me to a little room, where she had a snug pallet prepared for me, upon which I laid my weary limbs, and slept for some time. When I awoke, I had a raging fever, and soon became quite ill. For two weeks I laid in that house, hanging between life and death, and cared for with the kindness that parents bestow upon their children.

The most of that time I was quite delirious, talking incessantly of my family, and alluding to the trying scenes I had passed through. When I became conscious, I felt comparatively comfortable, and quite free from pain. It was some time, however, before I could realize my situation; for it seemed to me that I had just awoke from some horrible dream. But, as I gazed around the room, memory returned. I could hardly think it possible that I should receive such tender care in South Carolina. I was in a good bed, the room looked comfortable, and all the appliances of faithful nursing were around me; and this, too, in a locality where I expected neither charity nor mercy.

I was not suffered to meditate long upon my situation, however, before the old gentleman came up to see me. As he stood over me, I opened my eyes, and saw his countenance beaming with evident satisfaction.

"I am glad to see you looking better, Mr. Harrold," he said.

"I feel better, sir; but I am very weak."

"I do not wonder. But who is Caroline you spoke of so often? You were out of your mind, and used that name frequently, with others."

"That is my wife's name," I replied; and then I began to comprehend the extent of my illness. "Oh, sir," I exclaimed, "how can I ever repay your kindness to me? You have saved my life. Here I am, far from home, among those from whom, according to the discipline of war, I have no right to expect this generous treatment." He interrupted, by saying—

"Mr. Harrold, you are no enemy of ours. We had nothing to do with this war. They (meaning the secessionists) held a convention in Sumpter District, and only two old men attended it from this locality. They opposed the extreme measures advocated by the more impetuous rebels, as far as they could with safety, but there was so much excitement that none heeded their warning. These elderly gentlemen argued against hasty proceedings, and counselled patience, until President Lincoln should commit some overt act. For this advice, they were seriously threatened, and were told, as they valued their lives, not to say one word against secession. Indeed, some of the more reckless threatened to blow their brains out. They, with a number of others, were compelled to acquiesce in the proceedings, or leave the convention as marked men."

Such was the state of affairs before the outburst of the rebellion, as related by my old father and benefactor. The reader may judge of my astonishment when I heard such language from a son of the Palmetto State. Nor was this feeling confined to this particular section. I learned that there was by no means a unanimous feeling in favor of secession; but the influence and activity of the leading politicians, added to the clamor of a large class of idle and worthless young men, who shirked the war as much as possible when the fighting commenced, bore down all opposition. Thousands were thus dragged into the vortex of treason, because it was dangerous to both life and property to raise a voice against popular sentiment.

Reflecting upon the jeopardy in which I might

place him, and not knowing what disposition he might make of me, I said—

"Well, sir, you have done everything that a father could do for me, and I do not want to get you into any trouble on my account."

"Make yourself easy about that. I will tell you more," he continued. "The leading men, in stirring up this war, came through this neighborhood making speeches—declaring that not a drop of blood would be shed. Senator James Chesnut asserted over and over again that he would drink all the blood that secession might cause to be shed. These harangues pictured a golden future to the South, and completely turned the popular tide in their favor, because none dared to present a reverse view of the question. Of course, the minority had no alternative but submission.

"After they commenced the war, every ablebodied man was conscripted—my two sons among them. (The old man paused with emotion, and the tears streamed down his furrowed cheeks.) They were both taken from me; and while deprived of their assistance, we are compelled to give one-tenth of the little we can raise ourselves to the Confederacy, and haul it to a specified depôt, without one cent of compensation."

"Sir," said I, "this is cruel—awful!"

"So give yourself no concern about compromising me. There are none around me but very old men—

all others are conscripted; and we have no Confederate officials within many miles of us."

My heart was overflowing with gratitude, and I again exclaimed—

"Oh, my benefactor, how can I ever reward you for this manifestation of kindness—this noble generosity toward one who has no claims upon you?"

"Never mind that. The only danger of discovery may arise from hunting parties scouring the woods, which you must avoid in daylight. A number of such are continually prowling about in search of deserters. They hunt them down with dogs."

"What! hunt deserters with dogs?"

"Yes, indeed; that is a common occurrence."

"Are there many deserters?"

"Yes,—any quantity of them in the woods and swamps."

CHAPTER XVII.

RECUPERATING—RESUMING MY TRADE—WAR PRICES AT THE SOUTH.

I soon began to gain strength under the tender nursing of her who was acting a mother's part by me. At the end of three weeks I could walk about quite smart. Some of the neighbors visited me, all of whom appeared to be sensible, hospitable people; and I found their sentiments accorded with those expressed by the old gentleman. They seemed to take great pleasure in having me detail incidents of the war, and were much interested in the accounts I gave them of the North—such as particulars in regard to wealth, population, general resources, and the progress of private enterprise and public improvements.

I found this to be a very sparse settlement, with neighbors few and far between. The major part of them were related to my old friend by blood or marriage, and he was recognized as the patriarch of the locality. This may account, in a great measure, for the unanimity of sentiment in regard to the rebellion, as he was justly conceded to be the oracle of the neighborhood.

As I gained strength, I tried to make myself

useful,—hoping to repay, in ever so small a measure, the kindness that had been lavished upon me. Every morning I went out with the old gentleman and assisted him to feed his little stock of cattle, sheep, hogs, &c. I confess I never before saw such diminutive animals. He had some three or four cattle, and I have no doubt a strong man could have carried any one of them. The hogs were proportionately small, scrubby and thriftless. The feed consisted of corn-blades and peas for the cattle and sheep, and corn for the hogs.

I would rise very early in the morning, feed the stock, make fence, or do anything that I thought would add to the interest of the family. I sought every opportunity to repair and fix up little things in and around the house, which could add to the convenience or comfort of the old folks; and they appeared much interested in my manner and mode of doing such work, as it was so different from Southern customs. The old man complimented me by saying that I was the smartest white man he ever saw.

Being still barefooted, I looked around for some material that would answer as a substitute for shoes. I saw an old tan-trough hewed out of a large pine log, and inquired if they had any leather; for I saw they were both badly off for shoes. I told them I was a shoemaker, and would fit them out if I could obtain material.

"I have a young cowhide tanned," said he, "and a lot of coon skins."

"Coon skins!" I exclaimed; "what kind of leather can you make out of them?"

"First rate," said he; and soon several were laid out before me. "There are some sorry ones among them, but a few that are good."

I examined them, and was surprised at their pliability and toughness.

"Now," said I, "have you anything to make them up with?"

"Oh, there's the rub. I have not."

I set my wits at work to supply the deficiency. I had procured a piece of maple wood, hewed out a last for each of them, and one for a daughter who lived with them, whose husband was conscripted. The lasts made, I got them to spin me some fine cotton thread. So far so good; but where was the wax to come from? I could not endure defeat for the want of so trifling, yet indispensable an article, so I procured some gum from a pine tree, put it in boiling water, added some grease, and made a most excellent wax. The pegs I made out of the maple. I then cut out patterns, and made the old folks and the daughter each a good pair of shoes.

For the edification of the trade, I will state that this task was accomplished with rather novel tools. I had to use an old broken blade of an awl—refitted to a handle,—my whetstone was a soft brick, and, with the exception of a case knife and hammer, these were the sole implements of my trade. I also made the daughter an additional pair of coon-hide shoes. When I had them all finished, the old man examined them critically, and exclaimed—"Well, I believe the Yankees are the smartest people in the world."

I procured an old pair of bootlegs for myself, and made up quite a decent pair of shoes, which I put on my feet with no little pride. All this was soon known throughout the settlement, and it was not long before I had plenty of work, all of which I made up for the benefit of my benefactors. The following is the list of prices he charged, when he found the material:—

<blockquote>
For a pair of shoes, men's wear............ $30.00
For a pair of shoes, women's wear. 20.00
Half-soleing, or foxing..................... 18.00
</blockquote>

Other work, including every description of repairing, was charged in proportion.

"Why, sir," said I, "you could nearly buy a case of shoes at the North for what you charge for a single pair."

"Well, what do you think I paid for my boys' shoes?"

"If I am governed by your charges, I should say fifty dollars."

"I paid ninety-five dollars for them in Camden."

"Your money cannot be worth much, then."

"I don't know; but such is our currency under the Confederacy."

I continued to work on, and to make myself useful indoors and out,—confining myself pretty close to the house, however, through the day. In the evening, I felt myself more at liberty, and frequently accompanied the old gentleman, who assured me of safety, saying—"There is nothing in the world to bring them here, unless they come in search of deserters." That accursed stockade had such terrors for me, that I could not feel secure a moment.

There was another anxiety preying upon my mind. I did not know how to get a letter to my family. I was very anxious to apprize them of my safety, as I knew it would relieve them of very unpleasant apprehensions. I concluded to write a letter to my wife, and inclose it to the Commissioner of Exchange, in Richmond, Virginia, as though coming from Florence, S. C. I did so, and my benefactor took it to Camden, S. C., twenty miles distant. My wife received that letter, which was the first knowledge of my whereabouts she obtained during the past seven months. I need not say what joy it gave them at home to know that I was alive and well, with a lively hope of meeting them again at no distant day.

CHAPTER XVIII.

SHERMAN ADVANCING—A FRIENDLY CONTRABAND—THE RESCUE—MY BENEFACTOR'S KINDNESS APPRECIATED.

I now began to turn my attention to General Sherman, whose advance was known to many in the neighborhood. I became strongly impressed with the belief that he would yet be my deliverer. Of course, we had no authentic information of his movements, but rumor was busy, and no doubt the panic he created caused the inhabitants to fear his approach every hour. I became acquainted with a negro in the neighborhood, who sympathized with me very warmly, and who kept me posted in regard to the movements of our own and the rebel forces,—that is, he would tell it to me as it was told to him; but he appeared to have pretty accurate information of General Sherman and his army. He met me one evening, and appeared to be overjoyed.

"Massa Harrold," said Bob, (for that, I believe, was all of his name,) "I hearn dat massa Sherman got Sabannah."

"Is that so, Bob?"

"I's hearn it, sartin."

"I hope so with all my heart."

"Dey do say he's comin' to Souf Carlina. If he does, I's gwine wid 'im, shoah."

"So shall I, Bob;" but I little thought it was coming to pass so soon.

My benefactor informed me that he heard Mr. Sherman, as the Southerners invariably called him, had captured Savannah, and that he would continue his march through South Carolina. If ever I fervently prayed for anything, I did for that event. There were a great many reports in regard to his movements, and, judging from the wide-spread panic which existed, I concluded that he could not be very far off. Finally, we received positive information that he had crossed the line, and was now upon the "sacred soil" of South Carolina. The excitement soon became intense. There was not a boy from fifteen years and upwards, or a man from sixty to seventy years of age, but was compelled to turn out and perform patrol duty.

News came that a tremendous battle was expected to come off at Branchville, about seventy miles distant from us. Several hundred negroes, my aged friend informed me, were throwing up entrenchments, and every preparation was being made to give that famous flanking general a warm reception. But when he got ready to move, that stern rebel-driver gave them the slip, cut them off from Columbia, and, one fine morning, made his appearance before what they designed to be the capital of the rickety Confederacy.

I was soon informed, by my old friend, that Columbia had fallen. Oh, what glorious news to me. My heart fairly leaped with joy. Only fifty miles from me!

"What shall I do?" was my first inquiry.

"You might try to reach them," said my old friend; "but, remember, the Confederates are between you and Mr. Sherman. It is reported, however, that he is going to Charlotte, North Carolina."

I was sadly perplexed—almost to agony. I knew not what to do. We heard no more of General Sherman's movements for three or four days. My suspense was intolerable, so much so, that I could scarcely sleep or eat. At length Bob, my negro friend, approached me one evening, in great excitement—

"Massa Harrold, I hearn you cavalry come into Camden las' night."

"O, Bob, that cannot be. The old gentleman has not heard a word of it yet."

"I tells you I hearn it, sartin."

"God grant it, Bob," said I, most fervently.

"I's ready to go—all de niggers in de country is gwine."

"So am I, Bob."

Next morning, my old friend informed me that he had heard some Yankee cavalry had made their appearance in the vicinity of Camden, which is only thirty-five miles from Columbia. All such information only tended to increase my suspense, although each rumor cheered me, and gave me new hope; but I kept as calm as possible, under the circumstances, deeming it prudent not to distress my aged friends by useless repinings.

While sitting in my little room, trying to control my feelings, I heard the tramp of horses through the woods. I immediately sprang to the window, and beheld a horseman approaching dressed in a rebel lieutenant's uniform.

"Great God!" I exclaimed, "I am betrayed."

I dropped down in a chair almost overcome with terror, and despair took the place of hope. While bewailing my sad fate, and expecting a speedy return to the horrors of the prison-pen, I heard a voice inquire—

"Is there a Yankee prisoner here?"

Again I went to the window, and cautiously looked out, when I saw another man in Yankee uniform. Although I was still suffering from my back and hips, I bounded over the little stairway, and rushing out to the man in rebel uniform, asked—

"Are you a Yankee?"

"Yes, I am."

The scene that followed beggars description. It would be impossible to act my part over again. I laughed, cried, hurrahed, and hugged first one then the other. I was nearly crazed with joy; for it was

5*

the first certain evidence offered me of my deliverance from danger.

My poor old benefactor stood by me in great terror, not knowing what might be the consequences to him. My first impulse, however, admonished me to ask protection for him, and hastily explained the heavy obligations he had placed me under. The soldier in rebel uniform spoke to him kindly, and told him to make himself perfectly easy, no harm should come to him after the noble part he had acted toward a Union soldier.

The cavalrymen were piloted to the house by a negro, who was apprised of my flight and concealment. It is astonishing to know how soon and how wide-spread any matter relating to the progress of the war becomes diffused among the negroes. I have not a doubt that my hiding-place was known to them in a circumference of twenty miles or more, and that had I been betrayed, I should have been warned in time to escape.

I inquired where our troops were, and was informed that they were not over half a mile in the rear—the cavalry being in advance of the command.

"What cavalry is it?" I inquired.

"The 7th Illinois and 29th mounted Missouri Infantry."

"Do you belong to them?"

"No; like yourself, I am an escaped prisoner."

"What regiment do you belong to?"

"The 6th Pennsylvania cavalry."

"Is it possible! I know several in that regiment. What is your position?"

"Captain," he replied.

"So I am indebted to Captain Hazel, Colonel Rush's Lancers, for my rescue,—both of them brave officers and true gentlemen.

I was so anxious to see our men, that I begged the privilege of going forward to meet them. Captain Hazel and myself started off for that purpose, leaving his companion to stay with my friends as a guard against any molestation. About a quarter of a mile from the house, we saw some half dozen men emerging from the woods. When I beheld the blue coats once more, I was almost transported with delight. I rushed toward them, and hugged the first man I met, embracing several in turn. This strange proceeding on my part quite surprised the men, and I heard one of them remark, "What is the matter with that fellow? Is he crazy?" Some of them, at first, thought I was a rebel prisoner, until they witnessed my joyous demonstrations. This command consisted of the two regiments already named, being the advance of General Logan's corps.

It is proper to remark that this portion of our troops were the outscouts which General Sherman made a practice of keeping well out on his right and left, to scour the country on both sides of the main body of the army. This was done to prevent surprise, to collect provisions, procure forage, and to make what he styled "an impression upon the country." They were known among the "boys" as "Sherman's bummers." He ordered every rebel who could handle a musket to be taken as a prisoner; and these duties required a divergence of many miles from the great body of the troops.

When I told my comrades that I was an escaped prisoner, they greeted me with the most brotherly affection. I was taken to the head-quarters of the two regiments, commanded by a major. When I beheld the old flag, I embraced the staff that bore the proud emblem of our nationality. I never was particularly demonstrative in moments of excitement, but, on this occasion, I was nearly beside myself, and must have given but sorry evidence of a sound mind. In my weak condition, this sudden transition from wretchedness to the very fullness of joy, was too great a tax upon my strength. I sank under it, and was borne from the flag-staff to the major's head-quarters, where every kindness was lavished upon me, until I grew more composed. I knew that I had the warm sympathy of the brave fellows who stood around me, for several evinced it by tears as well as by word and act.

Some, perhaps, may think this picture overdrawn; but had they felt and suffered as I had, and endured the same torture, in an almost hopeless effort to escape—oppressed by despondency, and yearning to embrace wife and children—they would scarcely have been less expressive. I profess to have a reasonable share of self-control, and am seldom over-impulsive; but this good fortune—this happy deliverance—came so unexpected that I could not restrain my joy. Had I been found by Union soldiers in the condition I was in when the old gentleman first saw me, and taken within the lines, I do not think I could have survived, for my system was too much exhausted to have endured the excitement and wild rapture which my safety inspired.

I requested the Major to furnish my benefactor a guard, which he promptly stationed at the house, and I remained with my friends all night. Next morning the Fourth Division, commanded by Gen. Coarse, came up, about 9 o'clock. I was advised by the Major, who commanded the cavalry, to apply to the General for a guard to relieve his men, as he had to move forward. I went with my old friend to Gen. Coarse, and informed him of all the circumstances connected with my case. He promptly furnished me with a guard of three men, and congratulated me on my escape. He also told the old man that he would not be the loser for having treated a Union soldier kindly. He then asked my friend if he had any horses or mules. He told the General he had neither. (The one he rode when I was found in the woods belonged to a neighbor.) An officer was immediately sent to the Provost Marshal's Office, with orders to let him have a horse or a mule if he had any. In a short time my aged friend was presented with a splendid mule.

In consequence of the heavy rains, Lynch's creek was very much swollen. The water was so high that we were compelled to stop two days—encamped within a quarter of a mile of my old friend's house. He was supplied with an abundance of coffee, sugar and other necessaries—luxuries to which he had long been a stranger. I was more than gratified to see his kindness so handsomely appreciated by Gen. Coarse and all under his command. It was but a partial return for his generosity, at least, although my individual obligations are none the less.

CHAPTER XIX.

THE PARTING—"HOMEWARD BOUND"—THE MARCH—
EXODUS OF NEGROES—ARRIVAL AT CHERAW.

I parted from that aged couple and their daughter as a son would part from parents and sister. I confess a shade of sadness came upon me as I was about to leave them, for they had given me evidence of affection that far transcended the instincts of humanity; and I can truly say, they were entwined around my heart with feelings of love and gratitude that will cling to me while life lasts. I need not describe that tearful farewell—indeed, I could not. It was such as the reader can more readily imagine under the circumstances; but I do think the parting blessing of that aged couple inspired me with a deeper reverence for old age, and reminded me of the patriarchs of old, when they piously laid their hands upon the first born, and devoutly uttered the words—"bless thee, my son." I may never meet them on earth again, but, if not, my prayer is, that I shall see them in the world to come, where I hope they will reap the full reward of good deeds performed here below.

As in the case of Mr. Outlaw, I hesitated to give publicity to the name of my benefactor; but, for the same reasons, I will state, that the man who acted a father's part by me was Mr. JAMES IRVIN KING, a gentleman universally esteemed and respected in the district in which he lived.

In view of this gentleman's kindness to me, and his frank expression of hostility to the rebellion, I could not, and cannot now, think the less of him, because his two sons were fighting against us in the rebel army. Thousands, like him, were forced to yield to the torrent of passion, which swept the willing and the unwilling alike into the confederate ranks, and from which he was only saved by his advanced years and Gen. Sherman's rapid advance; for, as that General approached the borders of South Carolina, an order was issued which would soon have his gray hairs beside the boy of fifteen in the ranks. Well I know that, in his inmost soul, he has been ready to exclaim, with the poet:

"Oh, pity, GOD, this miserable age!
What stratagems, how fell, how butcherly,
Erroneous, mutinous, and unnatural,
This deadly quarrel daily doth beget."

My cavalry friends desired me to travel with them, but my health would not admit of it. I was too weak to stand the fatigue. While loitering near one of the regiments I was approached by several men, who questioned me very closely, evidently with the suspicion that I was a rebel; and some of them imagined that the clothes I had on, being home-spun, such as are made in the rural districts, fully confirmed their suspicions. But, when I briefly related my adventures to them, they insisted upon my seeing their captain. I was soon introduced to him, and again rehearsed my adventures to as many as could get around me. This officer, who took charge of me, was Captain David C. Gamble, Company E, 66th Illinois Regiment; and to him and his men I am greatly indebted for many acts of kindness and tender care, during our march through South and North Carolina. He put me in a mess with his non-commissioned officers, close to his head-quarters.

I was furnished with a fine little animal to ride upon, and was assigned a position between the Surgeon and Sergeant-major, in the rear of the regiment. We started through a vast wilderness of woods, and marched until nearly sundown. We encamped, as was the custom of this army, where fence rails and water were most convenient. One of my mess, an intimate friend from New Jersey, who took a deep interest in me, would take my horse and "strike out" on a foraging expedition. He generally returned with a supply of poultry, canned fruit, and other luxuries. I never lived so well in all my life, as we had any quantity of provisions on the route. Although the mass of the people were greatly impoverished, we exacted tribute from the more wealthy, who were husbanding their resources with the utmost care.

Gen. Sherman, in this expedition, started out to

feed upon the country through which he passed. He kept mounted foragers in advance of his army, as well as upon each side of the main body, "gobbling up" everything in the shape of an animal, poultry, grain, or anything else that the people could subsist on. The object was to destroy all resources necessary to keep an army in the field. It seems like an inhuman mode of warfare to bring starvation upon an enemy, but it is an agent of success used by all contending armies.

It was about this time that Gen. Howard, commander of the 15th and 17th Corps, issued an order to kill all bloodhounds wherever found. Nothing pleased me better than to know that these instruments of pursuit and torture to runaway negroes and escaping prisoners were to be exterminated. Wolves in Russia inspire no more terror in that cold region than do bloodhounds at the South. More than one poor fugitive, I fear, fleeing from starvation as I did, were hunted down and torn in pieces by these dangerous brutes.

We maintained a steady, onward move, scarcely meeting any resistance. The rebels undertook to make a stand at a place called Flat Rock, in Kershaw District, but they were scattered and driven like dust before the wind, by Sherman's hosts. We moved on—leaving nothing but desolation in our track—sweeping an area of some 50 miles wide. We halted within 40 miles of Florence to build "corduroy" roads, and some 600 of "Sherman's bummers" made an unsuccessful attempt to rescue what prisoners remained at that place, but were outnumbered by the rebels, who kept a force of 3,000 there to guard the prison pen. The expedition, however, brought in about 100 prisoners, captured on the route.

We pushed on as fast as the condition of the country would admit, followed by long processions of negroes, of all ages and sexes, from the babe at the breast to feeble old age. They could be counted by thousands, carrying all manner of parcels. Many of them took possession of their masters' wagons and carriages, which were drawn by abandoned Government mules. These vehicles were loaded down with every description of trumpery, some of which was scarcely worth firewood. It was the greatest sight I ever beheld, and every hour seemed to add to the throng. A few stayed behind who could not overcome home attachments, and the parting between them and those who were "bound for freedom," was often truly affecting. In view of the result, it would have been far better had they all remained, as the vast number who followed the army suffered many privations. It was impossible to feed, with anything like regularity, such an immense number of camp followers, and thousands, by hardships and exposure, died, or reaped the seeds of disease that led to premature death.

Onward we marched, through swamps, bogs and

woods, overcoming every difficulty, until we drew near to Cheraw. While approaching this place we heard the booming of cannon. It was Gen. Kilpatrick "touching up" the rebel army, while retreating across the Pee Dee River. Finally, that old town was discerned in the distance, and I felt buoyant and happy to know I was drawing near to the place I had started out to reach, when hunted as a fugitive. In a short time I was riding through it in triumph, with the glorious stars and stripes waving proudly at the head of the column.

CHAPTER XX.

A TERRIBLE EXPLOSION—WE CROSS THE BIG PEE DEE—ARRIVAL AT FAYETTEVILLE, N. C.—DEPARTURE FOR WILMINGTON—THE START FOR HOME!—THE STORM.

We encamped in the vicinity of the town for some three days, until everything was in readiness for a forward movement. There I had the pleasure of seeing, for the first time, that great and glorious chieftain—that idol of the Western Army—Gen. W. T. Sherman. God bless him! and give him a long life of usefulness to his country. The "boys" loved him, and would have followed him through fire and water. This, in my opinion, is one of the secrets of his great success. *He had the affection of his men*, because he treated them like human beings. This, added to the indisputable military talent he displayed, gave his soldiers unlimited confidence in him as a commander, "because," they said, "he can always bring us out of the wilderness."

Everything in readiness, we took up our line of march through the town, halting in one of the main streets. While looking into a store which had been hastily abandoned, a terrible explosion took place about the distance of a square from me. The shock was awful—stunning—lifting me clear of the ground. Some four or five poor fellows of the 81st Ohio were literally blown to atoms, wounding in a shocking manner a number of others. The mangled remains of these unfortunate soldiers, and the surrounding ruins, presented a heart-sickening sight, such as I should be loth to look upon again. How strange it is, that men can walk over the mangled remains of their comrades in battle with but little, if any, emotion, and yet manifest the deepest sympathy, and almost shed tears, over a scene like this.

The remains of the poor fellows, or what was found of them, were deposited in a neighboring burying ground, where lie those of General Marion, the "Swamp Fox" of Revolutionary fame. Had they fallen in battle, it might have palliated the grief of relatives and friends at home to know that they had died nobly battling for the right; but such a death was well calculated to awaken the most poignant grief. They fell, however, in the line of duty, and will be honored none the less. It seems there were some twenty tons of powder in a neighboring building, through which some of the soldiers carelessly passed with a lighted segar—hence the explosion.

After the confusion and excitement incident to this sad calamity had subsided, we pursued our way across the Big Pee Dee River, started on our march, and struck the line of the old North State in about two hours. We had a great many difficulties to encounter in this section of country, having to build "corduroy" roads through immense swamps and forests, foraging, &c., as we moved onward, but living luxuriously.

At last Fayetteville hove in sight, and we soon encamped near that ancient town, where a consultation was held between the military and civil authorities at head-quarters, to decide upon some plan of disposing of the immense number of negroes and refugees who had followed us. It was a terrible blow to the darkies when they ascertained that a large number of them were to be left there. They were impressed with the belief that they were on their direct way to the North, where they hoped for a new existence. As their subsequent sufferings in this place has been a subject of newspaper comment, I need not allude to it here.

It was here that I bid farewell to my kind friend, Captain David C. Gamble. I feel under many obligations to him for his brotherly treatment throughout that long march, for which I shall never cease to feel grateful. I must also allude to the kindness of several of my messmates, among whom I would mention Lemuel Trowbridge, Thomas Wagner, John Freeman, and others, who endeared themselves to me by those acts of generosity and tender solicitude for my comfort, which can only spring from humane hearts. To these, I must add the chief surgeon and his gentlemanly assistants, who rendered me every professional and personal attention that kindness could suggest.

Captain Gamble gave me a note to the Provost Marshal of the 15th Corps, who procured me transportation from Fayetteville to Wilmington, N. C., on a rebel steamer, in company with a number of escaped prisoners and refugees. Homeward bound! Free, and among friends! The rebellion in its death-throes—our army victorious everywhere—the Union preserved as a whole—the stars and stripes waving in triumph! These were a few of the cheering thoughts that sent a thrill of joy to my heart.

And here it seems appropriate to give my readers a description of the closing scenes of the war, so eloquently portrayed by Mr. Osceola Lewis, in his "History of the 138th Regiment, Pennsylvania Volunteer Infantry," of which I was a member:—

"On the morning of April 3d, our victorious troops marched through the streets of the "Gate City" and those of Richmond, the long-disputed goal of protracted, tedious, and bloody campaigns, while Lee's army was making the best of an ignominious retreat into south-western Virginia. Close pursuit by our forces was made at once, and continued by way of Amelia Court House, until on the 6th, about sixteen miles west of the latter place, the enemy was brought to a stand, and Longstreet's and Ewell's rebel commands were fought by the 6th Corps and Sheridan's cavalry, with some co-operation from the 2d Corps, under General Humphrey's.

The field chosen by the enemy was well suited to the emergency, being an elevated position, overlooking a marshy bottom coursed by a stream known as Sailor's Creek. To reach the rebels, our troops were forced to cross this difficult space and ascend the eminence beyond in face of a galling fire.

The 1st and 3d Divisions of the 6th Corps were the only infantry commands closely engaged, and they, with two Divisions of Cavalry, attacked, fought and drove an enemy of greater strength from advantageous ground, and captured prisoners to an extent exceeding their own numbers.

Here again the 138th and 6th Maryland regiments fought side by side, and made a charge which opened this battle. The troops had marched about sixteen miles on the 6th, and from 3 P. M. till dusk took part in fighting as spirited and severe as any they had before experienced.

The rebels contended stubbornly, but our soldiers, buoyed by the great successes already arrived at, and knowing that an opportunity was here presented, strove with all their might to make it a finishing stroke, which was virtually effected, for it was the last important passage at arms of the campaign which finished the rebellion. It was willed by Providence that it should be the last fiery ordeal to be experienced by the 138th Regiment, and conscious of having given substantial aid in the advancement of the grand result, we inscribed on our roll of honor last but not least (neither to the soldier nor to the cause) the battle of Sailor's Creek. The men who fought it will not forget the presence of "Phil Sheridan," Wright, Seymour, and Keifer, and how well they did their duty; neither will they fail to rememher the weary march, the hasty formation, the sudden charge, the awful swamp, the staggering shock, the wavering pause, the last desperate onset, and the flight and capture of an enemy, who, gathering together trooper and foot-soldier, marine and seaman, armed with sabre and rifle, carbine and cutlass, strove in the "last ditch" to render more inglorious an infamous cause, and failing, with loss of property, blood and honor, went reeling to his final fall."

We left Fayetteville at 5 o'clock, P. M., about the 11th day of March, 1865, and arrived at Wilmington on the 12th at 10, A. M. After remaining there three or four days, we got transportation to Fortress Monroe, in the steamer J. S. Green. She left her moorings on the 16th of March, and soon got out to sea. As we approached Cape Hatteras the wind commenced blowing very hard, increasing in violence until night, when we experienced one of those terrible gales peculiar to that coast. A gale would scarcely express the force and power of the wind—it was a hurricane. The vessel was tossed about as though she was a mere mote upon the waters; and what rendered our situation more perilous, the crew were all sick, leaving only the captain, engineer and first mate fit for duty.

I never expected to see daylight. The sea was lashed to a perfect fury. The timbers of the vessel creaked as if strained to their utmost endurance, and the vessel labored as though she were a thing of life, and felt the responsibility of saving the precious lives on board. I became very despondent when I reflected upon the many dangers and trials through which I passed,—perhaps to meet a watery grave when hope was highest, and when so near the home I yearned to reach. Could it be possible that I was to perish after all, and never again behold my wife and children? I confess to more real fear on that occasion than I ever felt while marching into battle. It was certainly the darkest hour of my life, and I shall never forget the feelings of utter despair which the awful scene inspired.

But, a watchful Providence was over us. He brought us out of our tribulation. The steamer was kept steadily before the wind, and she obeyed her helm handsomely. Before morning the storm began to subside, and hope revived. We reached Fortress Monroe in safety, truly thankful for our preservation.

I took passage from this place to Baltimore on board a steamer, and procured transportation from that city to Washington, where I reported, with about twenty-five others, to the Commissary General of prisoners.

CHAPTER XXI.

HOME AGAIN!

After waiting some three or four days to get our affairs with the Government straightened up, I received my transportation home; and, on the evening of the 25th of March, arrived in Philadelphia. From the time I entered the cars until I reached my destination, I could scarcely contain myself. I was restless, nervous, and nearly wild with excitement, yet experiencing emotions of joy that I cannot well express. I reviewed all my perilous adventures, and could scarcely realize that I was safe, and would soon embrace my wife and children. It seemed to me to be a sudden transition from death to life.

Leaving the depot at Broad and Prime streets, I at once proceeded to my brother's house, in the city. My knock at the door was speedily answered. The scene that ensued I am incapable of describing. A brother embraced a brother whom he had long mourned as dead; for no word had come from me since I wrote the Camden letter, and all my relatives and friends had come to the conclusion that I had died, or was again captured and undergoing a lingering death. The people of the North had become better informed of the horrors incident to a Southern prison-pen; and although it is impossible to exaggerate them, a pretty correct idea was entertained of their life-destroying discipline. Indeed, it was remarkable that so many came out of them alive.

Tears of happiness came to our relief; and after we became more composed, I ventured to inquire, in a tremulous voice, after my wife and children. Oh! what if *one* of that dear flock should be missing! But, worse than all, what if the wife and mother should be snatched from me while absent! It was a moment of inexpressible anxiety. But ah, what a happy relief, when my brother informed me that they were all—*all*—alive and well.

Now my joy was most complete, save the unavoidable delay of meeting my family until Monday, as the train did not go down to Atlantic City on Sunday. But the certainty of joining them so soon made me content to wait, and I thanked God that they had been preserved to me. I felt that I was about to be rewarded for all my trials and sufferings.

On the morning of the 27th of March, 1865, I took the cars on the Camden and Atlantic Railroad for Atlantic City. I was on my way HOME! Oh, what magic in that word *home*—the goal for which I had labored, struggled, suffered and wept for so many long months, after an absence of two years. Time passed at a sluggish gait—never did cars move so slow. I could scarcely control my impatience.

As we neared Atlantic City I was left alone in

the car I occupied, the remainder of the passengers having been left by the way. I reached the depôt, however, in a state of nervous excitement, not knowing the residence my family then occupied. While still sitting in the cars, I heard a rush of boys toward the entrance, and the two foremost, on opening the door, simultaneously cried out, "My pappy!"

One I recognized, the other I did not. The next moment a female form came into the car and sprang toward me. I need not say that it was my beloved wife, and that I clasped her to me in one long embrace. For some moments neither of us could speak. But I will draw a veil over the scene that followed. The reader can imagine the caresses, the endearing words, the joy, with which a husband and father was welcomed home to wife and children. My wife could scarcely control her feelings. Laughing and crying at the same time, she would exclaim to all we met—"Here he is—I've got him at last." And the boys, for several days, would inform strangers as well as friends of my arrival. "Father's come home," seemed to be their daily song.

When I reached home, and once more became composed, my strength began to fail very rapidly. I had been kept up by excitement and anxiety. That gone, I sunk to a very prostrate condition. Mine had long been but artificial strength, and now the reaction commenced. I lay under medical treatment for three months before I could gain strength to move about; and when I left my bed I was very feeble and completely broken down in health, never again to be repaired.

The exposure and hardships I endured left me but a wreck of my former self. Although I slowly improved in health, I am by no means the man I was, and still feel the effects of my imprisonment and starvation. I shall carry the marks of rebel cruelty to my grave, perhaps at no distant day.

I find I can no longer apply myself closely to my trade. Pain and weakness are sad drawbacks, and the only source from which I can derive a proper support for my family is proportionately limited. Necessity, however, compels me to pursue it, and I am content to bear my afflictions, since they were acquired in the path of duty. To have been an humble actor in the stirring scenes which put down rebellion and banished treason from the land, is a proud—a glorious—record; one that soothes the most acute pain, and adapts my wants to my means. I would scarcely exchange it for health, wealth and luxury. I feel that I did my duty in the glorious and successful effort to preserve this Union, and the highest in command did no more.

I cannot close this brief narrative, in justice to many warm friends, without alluding to the kindness they exhibited toward my family in my absence. They received many favors from persons upon whom we had no claims; for all of which I am truly grateful.

To Governor Curtin, of Pennsylvania, the country is largely indebted for his labors and efficiency, as well as his personal sacrifice of health and means, to save our glorious Union. Every man who shouldered a musket will look upon him as a benefactor; for he left nothing undone to make the hardships of war endurable, to relieve the sick and wounded, and to care for their families at home. Excelled by no executive, and equalled by few, he set an example that could not fail to inspire zeal and patriotism in the great American heart, and which served to bring to our ranks thousands of the hardy mountaineers and gallant yeomen of that noble State. Governor Curtin needs no prouder record on the page of history than that which will give a faithful detail of the services he rendered his country during the rebellion.

To Governor Joel Parker, also, and the State authorities, much praise is due for the assistance afforded the families of soldiers; and the troops of New Jersey owe to him a debt of gratitude for his provision for the sick and wounded, as well as for looking after the comfort of those in the field. The State Agency established in Washington gave great facilities for the reception of necessary comforts from the homes of the soldiers, and for communicating with their families, that could not have been obtained otherwise; and many a sad heart was cheered—many of the sick revived—by letters and articles of luxury forwarded to camp by Colonel Rafferty, the State Agent.

I must repeat, that I do not pretend to give a history of the battles in which I participated, nor of the events that gave prominence to the war, during my connection with the army. A soldier cannot take in the movements of a vast number of men at a glance like the general in command, who plans and directs. He can only speak of his immediate surroundings, and this is all I have attempted. I relate my own experience, and what I saw—nothing more.

I can, however, vouch for the truth of the details, as I know there were always too many witnesses present to attempt exaggeration. My desire is to preserve a record of my services for my children, and to give the reader some idea of the sufferings, perils and triumphs of war, from a soldier's standpoint. If I have succeeded in winning commendation for the brave men who perilled health and life for the preservation of this glorious Union, I shall be well compensated, aside from the gratification of assisting to cement "many in one" for all coming time.

JOHN HARROLD.

Atlantic City, N. J.

CONTENTS.

CHAPTER I.
Enlistment—Drilling—Picket Duty 7

CHAPTER II.
Active Duty—Flanked—The Countermarch—Battles of Wapping Heights, Kelly's Ford and Brandy Station, ... 10

CHAPTER III.
The Army Reorganized—General Grant takes Command—The Battles of the Wilderness—"On to Richmond!"—The Terrible Conflict at Coal Harbor 16

CHAPTER IV.
Promotion—Capture 23

CHAPTER V.
Starting for "Libby" 30

CHAPTER VI.
The Horrors of Libby Prison—The Food—The Vermin 33

CHAPTER VII.
A Move for Andersonville—Incidents of the Passage—Inhumanity of the Rebels—Woman's Sympathy 36

CHAPTER VIII.
Andersonville—The Prison Pen—Captain Wirz—A Scene of Misery. 42

CHAPTER IX.
Incidents of Prison Life—The Cartel—The "Dead Line" 45

CHAPTER X.
The Chances of Escape Considered—The Attempt Made—A Failure—Caught in the Act 56

CHAPTER XI.
Our Removal to Florence—Fallacious Hopes 60

CONTENTS.

CHAPTER XII.
Another Plan of Escape—We Resolve to "Run the Guards"—The Flight—Bloodhounds on our Track—Perils of our Situation—They Lose our Trail 62

CHAPTER XIII.
Life in Forest and Swamp—Precarious Subsistence—Help from an Unexpected Source 68

CHAPTER XIV.
Again on the Tramp—A Ruse—Another Period of Suffering and Privation 76

CHAPTER XV.
A Friendly Negro—Unexpected Meeting with a Planter—Another Timely Refuge 86

CHAPTER XVI.
A Severe Attack of Fever—Delirium—My Host's Opinion of the War—How it was Forced upon the People 92

CHAPTER XVII.
Recuperating—Resuming my Trade—War Prices at the South 97

CHAPTER XVIII.
Sherman Advancing—A Friendly Contraband—The Rescue—My Benefactor's Kindness Appreciated 102

CHAPTER XIX.
The Parting—"Homeward Bound"—The March—Exodus of Negroes—Arrival at Cheraw 111

CHAPTER XX.
A Terrible Explosion—We Cross the Big Pee Dee—Arrival at Fayetteville, N. C.—Departure for Wilmington—The Start for Home!—The Storm 117

CHAPTER XXI.
Home Again! 124

www.ingramcontent.com/pod-product-compliance
Lightning Source LLC
Chambersburg PA
CBHW031334160426
43196CB00007B/684